Brilliant Create your own Website

Rob Clymo

Harlow, England • London • New York • Boston • San Francisco • Toronto • Sydney • Singapore • Hong Kong
Tokyo • Seoul • Taipei • New Delhi • Cape Town • Madrid • Mexico City • Amsterdam • Munich • Paris • Milan

Pearson Education Limited
Edinburgh Gate
Harlow
Essex CM20 2JE
England

and Associated Companies throughout the world

Visit us on the World Wide Web at:
www.pearsoned.co.uk

First published 2007

ISBN: 978-0-13-204877-4

British Library Cataloguing-in-Publication Data
A catalogue record for this book is available from the British Library

10 9 8 7 6 5 4 3 2 1
11 10 09 08 07

Prepared for Pearson Education Ltd by Syllaba Ltd (http://www.syllaba.co.uk).
Typeset in 12pt Arial Condensed by 30
Printed and bound in Great Britain by Ashford Colour Press Ltd, Gosport.

The publisher's policy is to use paper manufactured from sustainable forests.

Brilliant guides

What you need to know and how to do it

When you're working on your computer and come up against a problem that you're unsure how to solve, or want to accomplish something in an application that you aren't sure how to do, where do you look? Manuals and traditional training guides are usually too big and unwieldy and are intended to be used as end-to-end training resources, making it hard to get to the info you need right away without having to wade through pages of background information that you just don't need at that moment – and helplines are rarely that helpful!

Brilliant guides have been developed to allow you to find the info you need easily and without fuss and guide you through the task using a highly visual, step-by-step approach – providing exactly what you need to know when you need it!

Brilliant guides provide the quick easy-to-access information that you need, using a detailed table of contents and troubleshooting guide to help you find exactly what you need to know, and then presenting each task in a visual manner. Numbered steps guide you through each task or problem, using numerous screenshots to illustrate each step. Added features include 'See also' boxes that point you to related tasks and information in the book, while 'Did you know?' sections alert you to relevant expert tips, tricks and advice to further expand your skills and knowledge.

In addition to covering all major office PC applications, and related computing subjects, the *Brilliant* series also contains titles that will help you in every aspect of your working life, such as writing the perfect CV, answering the toughest interview questions and moving on in your career.

Brilliant guides are the light at the end of the tunnel when you are faced with any minor or major task.

Author's acknowledgements

This book is dedicated to my Mum and Dad.

Publisher's acknowledgements

The author and publisher would like to thank the following for permission to reproduce the material in this book: 1&1 Internet Ltd, 123 Domain Names UK, AddMe LLC, Adobe Systems Incorporated, American Library Association, BBC, British Telecommunications plc., CoffeeCup Software, Inc., EasyByte Software, fantomaster.com, Google UK, Hit-Counter-Download.com, Htmlgames, Keynote NetMechanic, Lexico Publishing Group, LLC, MySpace, Nominet UK, Orange Home UK plc., Web CEO Ltd, Webeden, Website Pros, Worldwide Recipes, www.visitorcounters.org, Yahoo! Inc., ZyWeb Ltd.

Screen shots from Corel Paint Shop Pro X are Copyright 2005 Corel Corporation and Corel Corporation Limited, reprinted by permission.

Microsoft product screen shots reprinted with permission from Microsoft Corporation.

In some instances we have been unable to trace the owners of copyright material, and we would appreciate any information that would enable us to do so.

Special thanks to:

Geoff Spick for contributing Chapter 6: Creating a website using Expression Web Designer and material for page 192.

P.K. MacBride for permission to use material on pages 1–28, 41 and 190 which first appeared in his book *Brilliant Internet for the Over 50s*.

Lon Barfield of the Usability Design Partnership for contributing the Web Usability design tips in Chapter 7.

Dom Brookman for permission to use material on pages 39 and 40 which first appeared in his book *Brilliant Internet*.

Clare H, Clare C and Marissa for their help with child care.

About the author

A journalist for nearly two decades, Rob Clymo has spent the last five years dedicating his time to writing about web design and the internet. In that period he has been the editor of *Web Pages Made Easy* and *Website Maker* magazines and made regular freelance contributions to a host of other computing and technology publications. As well as specialising in writing beginner-friendly web design tutorials, Rob also makes regular forays into website construction himself. He has developed various eCommerce and database-driven sites and is currently a web developer for Bournemouth University. He spends his spare time building and maintaining online ventures for a handful of business clients.

Contents

Introduction

Welcome to *Brilliant Create your own Website*, a visual quick reference book that shows you how to establish and maintain your presence on the Web. Learn the basics of how to create a web page and how to design the layout to make it appropriate to your readers, how to set up a website and test it and, perhaps most importantly, how to get your site seen. We have focussed on describing software applications that are commonly used by amateur website developers (such as online services, FrontPage and Expression Web Designer – both found in the Microsoft Office suite, and Paint Shop Pro) rather than the expensive but powerful professional developer tools.

Find what you need to know – when you need it

You don't have to read this book in any particular order. We've designed the book so that you can jump in, get the information you need, and jump out. To find the information that you need, just look up the task in the table of contents or Troubleshooting guide, and turn to the page listed. Read the task introduction, follow the step-by-step instructions along with the illustration, and you're done. Please note that we have described how to create websites using various different software applications and, in order to avoid duplication of content, we have included numerous 'See also' cross references to point you to the section of the book that deals with a particular task.

How this book works

Each task is presented with step-by-step instructions and annotated screen illustrations on the same page. This arrangement lets you focus on a single task without having to turn the pages too often.

How you'll learn

Find what you need to know – when you need it

How this book works

Step-by-step instructions

Troubleshooting guide

Spelling

Step-by-step instructions

This book provides concise step-by-step instructions that show you how to accomplish a task. Each set of instructions includes illustrations that directly correspond to the easy-to-read steps. Eye-catching text features provide additional helpful information in bite-sized chunks to help you work more efficiently or to teach you more in-depth information. The 'For your information' feature provides tips and techniques to help you work smarter, while the 'See also' cross-references lead you to other parts of the book containing related information about the task. Essential information is highlighted in 'Important' boxes that will ensure you don't miss any vital suggestions and advice.

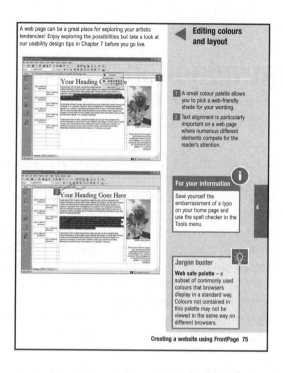

A web page can be a great place for exploring your artistic tendencies! Enjoy exploring the possibilities but take a look at our usability design tips in Chapter 7 before you go live.

◀ Editing colours and layout

1 A small colour palette allows you to pick a web-friendly shade for your wording.

2 Text alignment is particularly important on a web page where numerous different elements compete for the reader's attention.

For your information ⓘ

Save yourself the embarrassment of a typo on your home page and use the spell checker in the Tools menu.

Jargon buster

Web safe palette – a subset of commonly used colours that browsers display in a standard way. Colours not contained in this palette may not be viewed in the same way on different browsers.

Creating a website using FrontPage 75

Troubleshooting guide

This book offers quick and easy ways to diagnose and solve common problems that you might encounter using the Troubleshooting guide. The problems are grouped into categories that are presented alphabetically.

Spelling

We have used UK spelling conventions throughout this book. You may therefore notice some inconsistencies between the text and the software on your computer which is likely to have been developed in the USA. We have however adopted US spelling for the words 'disk', 'dialog' and 'program' as these are becoming commonly accepted throughout the world.

Troubleshooting guide

Creating your first website

Introduction

Building a website is not that difficult, as long as you don't need anything fancier than formatted text and images on the pages, with a straightforward set of links between them. The pages can be created from 'scratch' – writing the HTML code directly, which is far easier than you might at first expect. Of course, they can also be produced using a number of different applications, ranging from specialised multimedia editing suites to Word. In this chapter we will create a basic web page using HTML in order to demonstrate the fundamental construction techniques. Although you will probably choose to use a web authoring software package in the long run (they do all the coding for you and we describe how to use these later in the book), it is well worth understanding the code by which they operate. So we recommend starting with this chapter and experimenting briefly with the tags before you go on to explore other options. We will also touch briefly on creating a basic site using Word. In future chapters we will demonstrate how to make much 'fancier' sites using specialised software and providing design guidelines, but for now, let's get on with the basics.

Jargon buster

Website – a set of related web pages, usually owned and constructed by one organisation or individual. Navigational aids and hyperlinks allow the visitor to find their way around the site.

HTML – HyperText Markup Language, a system of instructions that browsers can interpret to display text and images.

What you'll do

Understand HTML tags

Create your own index page

View your index page

Understand the basics of text formatting

Format your text

Understanding the basics of setting colours

Set your colours

Set the text size

Draw a line

Make a list

Create hyperlinks

Understand the basics of displaying an image

Display an image

Link a thumbnail to an image

Link pages in a website

Create a web page in Word

Format text in Word

Create a link in Word

Follow links in Word

Understanding HTML tags

In HTML, all styling is done with tags – codes which tell the browser how to display text or images. These are mainly in pairs, one at each end of whatever is being styled. They follow simple rules:

- A tag is always enclosed in <angle brackets>.

- The opening and closing tags of each pair are identical except for a / before the identifier in the end tag.

- Tags can be written in either capitals or lower case.

- Tags can be on the same line as the enclosed text, or on separate lines – it makes no difference to the appearance in the browser.

For example, to get a third level heading – 14 point bold type – the tags are <H3> and </H3>. So you would write:

    <h3>This is a sub-head</h3>

or, remembering the last two rules, you could write it like this:

    <H3>
    This is a sub-head
    </H3>

Both produce this same effect:

This is a sub-head

Use whichever form is easiest to read in your text file.

Commonly used tags

    <HTML>…</HTML>

Mark the start and end of the HTML file.

    <HEAD>…</HEAD>

Mark the header area, that will hold the title and information about the page, which search engines can use to identify the nature and contents of the page.

The remainder of the text is the body and is enclosed by:

    <BODY>…</BODY>

This holds the code for the visible page.

    <TITLE>…</TITLE>

Whatever is marked as the title is displayed in the window's title bar.

See also

Instructions on pages 24 and 25 demonstrate how you can get Word to produce web pages directly – letting it write the tags for you.

Important

An HTML file is plain text, and can be created in any editor or word-processor that can output plan ASCII text – WordPad or Notepad (they should both be on the Accessories menu in Windows) are ideal.

Jargon buster

Web – World Wide Web, also shortened to WWW or W3. One of the most popular ways of using the internet, it consists of billions of web pages that can be viewed through browsers.

For your information

Keep up-to-date with developments in the HTML standard on the World Wide Web Consortium's website: www.w3.org.

Creating your own index page

The first page anyone meets on your site will be the index page (otherwise known as the Home page), so we'll start by creating that. We'll actually do this in stages. At first we will set up a very simple page, then come back later to add links to it so that you can move from the index page to the others once you have created them.

This is my page. Yours should have the same structure and tags, but with your own words for the title and heading.

1 Set up a new folder for your home page files. You will be saving all the pages and images here.

2 Start NotePad, WordPad, Word – whichever you prefer.

3 Type in the HTML text shown here, customised to suit you.

4 Open the File menu and select Save As…

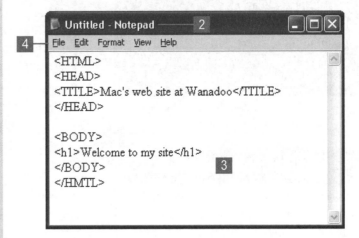

```
<HTML>
<HEAD>
<TITLE>Mac's web site at Wanadoo</TITLE>
</HEAD>

<BODY>
<h1>Welcome to my site</h1>
</BODY>
</HMTL>
```

See also

Advice on organising your files is given on page 38.

4

Jargon buster

Home page – the first page your browser loads when you type in the address or URL of a website. The 'gateway' or entrance to a site.

Index – the home page and entrance to your website. The first page to open when your web address is typed into a browser.

5 Locate your home page folder.

6 Save the document as a text file with the name 'index.htm'.

7 Click Save.

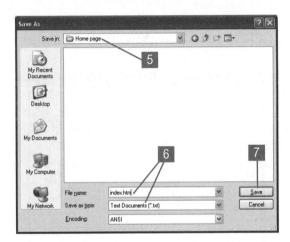

Important

Web page files can have .htm or .html extensions. Some Internet Service Providers insist that your top level page is called index.html – with an 'L'. Check the rules at your ISP.

Viewing your index page

In this early stage of construction, your 'website' will remain located on your computer, and you will be the only one who will be able to see it. Later, you will upload the completed pages and image files to your web space at your ISP's site – and then it will be on the web. Meanwhile, you can still view your pages in Internet Explorer.

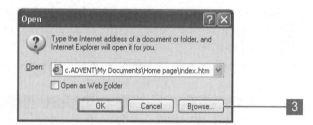

1 Switch to, or start Internet Explorer. You do not need to be online, but it won't matter if you are.

2 Open the File menu and select Open.

3 At the Open dialog box click Browse.

4 Look in the website folder and open your index.htm file.

5 Check the display and return to the editor to enhance and improve the text file!

Jargon buster

ISP – Internet Service Provider – organisation whose main business it is to enable people to access the internet.

Timesaver tip

It is quick and easy to see the effects of changes in your HTML file. Keep Internet Explorer and the editor windows open, and after each change to the text, save the HTML file again, then click on Refresh to reload the new version into Internet Explorer.

The simplest tags are the ones that format text. These will produce six levels of headings, a small, italicised style (mainly used for email addresses), and bold and italic for emphasis.

<H1>	</H1>	# Heading 1
<H2>	</H2>	## Heading 2
<H3>	</H3>	### Heading 3
<H4>	</H4>	**Heading 4**
<H5>	</H5>	**Heading 5**
<H6>	</H6>	**Heading 6**
<B>	</B>	**Bold**
<I>	</I>	*Italic*
<Address>	</Address>	*Small italic style*

The Heading and Address tags break the text up into separate lines, but untagged text appears as a continuous stream. Create separate paragraphs with these tags:

    <P></P>   Start a new paragraph with a space before and after.

    Start a new line without a space before it.

When a browser reads an HTML file, it ignores all spaces (apart from a single one between words), and [Enter] key presses. It doesn't matter how you lay out your HTML text – you can indent it, and add line breaks to make it easier to read, but it won't affect what your visitors see – only the tags affect the layout of the page in the browser.

Tags can sometimes be combined. For example, you can make text bold like this:

    <B>This is bold</B>

or make it italic like this:

    <I>This is italic</I>

or apply both bold and italics like this:

    <I><B>This is bold and italics</B></I>

When you combine tags, you must nest them – write one pair inside the other.

Timesaver tip

If your formatting tags don't seem to be doing the job properly, check that each opening <TAG> has a matching closing </TAG> – and that it is in the right place.

Formatting your text

1. Start a new file in your editor.

2. Type in the sample text shown opposite, replacing my words with yours if you like, but keeping the tags and the structure.

3. Save the file as 'text.htm'.

4. Switch to the Internet Explorer window and use the File, Open command to load in your new page.

5. Check for errors. Are there any typos in the text? Is it formatted as it should be?

6. If necessary, edit and resave the HTML file, then refresh the browser display.

Jargon buster

Browser – a software application especially designed for accessing and displaying the information in the web. This is also true the other way around: the web is an information system designed to be viewed on browsers.

```
<HTML>
<HEAD>
<TITLE>Formatting text</TITLE>
</HEAD>

<BODY>
<H1>Formatting text</H1>
<H2>Using header tags...</H2>
<H6>...though headers can be rather small</H6>
<BR>
And some plain text here after a break.
<P>and here using the paragraph tag to leave a space above
the paragraph</P>
<P>We can make things stand out in <B>bold</B> or
<I>italics</I> or <B><I>both</I></B></P>
<P>
<Address>This page was made by me</Address>
</BODY>
</HTML>
```

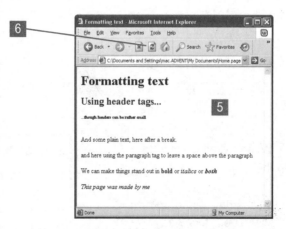

Important

Remember that Internet Explorer is not the only browser. Though all browsers can read and display HTML pages, there are some minor differences in how they interpret some HTML tags. Professional web builders always check the appearance of their sites on different browsers.

Colours can be defined in two ways. The simplest is to use standard colour names. All browsers, or any type and age, can recognise and respond to these names in HTML pages:

Black	Grey	White	Navy Blue
Blue	Green	Lime	Maroon
Red	Turquoise	Purple	Olive
Aqua	Fuchsia	Yellow	

Newer browsers can also interpret a wider range of colour names, but these should be enough for most purposes.

Colours can also be defined by the values of their Red, Green and Blue components – given in that order and in hexadecimal digits. These values can be anything from 00 to FF, but are best set at 00 (off), 80 (half/dark) or FF (full power/bright), e.g.:

FFFF00

gives Red and Green at full, with no Blue, resulting in Yellow. Combinations of 00, 80 and FF values should come out true on all screens. Intermediate values, giving more subtle shades of colours, may not always be displayed properly.

BODY colours

The BODY tag can have extra information written into it to set the colours of the background and

For your information

Instant Hex

All modern numbering systems are founded on 'place value' – how much a digit stands for depends upon its place in the figure. In base-10, 42 means $4 \times 10 + 2$. In hexadecimal, the place multiplier is 16 rather than 10. So 42 in hex is worth $4 \times 16 + 2 = 66$ in base-10. To make hex work, more digits are needed – 0 1 2 3 4 5 6 7 8 9 A B C D E F – with A to F standing for the values 10 – 15 in the base-10 system. Hex is used in computing because it is compact – you can represent any number from 0 to 255 in two digits ($FF = 15 \times 16 + 15 = 255$) – and because there is a simple conversion between hex and binary, the native numbering system of computer chips.

text of the page. The option keywords are BGCOLOR and TEXT and are set like this:

```
<BODY BGCOLOR = 'black' TEXT = 'white'>
```

FONT colours

At any point on the page, you can change the colour of the text with the tag:

```
<FONT COLOR = 'colour name'>
```

Understanding the basics of setting colours (cont.)

The colour is used for all following text until it is reset with another <FONT COLOR =...> tag. You can use it to pick out words within normal text – though you can get strange results if you use the tags inside Headings.

The closing </FONT> tag can be omitted. If you use it, the text colour will revert to what it was before the opening <FONT COLOR =...> tag.

Did you know?

You must have a good contrast in shade – as well as in hue – between your text colours and the background colour. If they are too close together the page will be hard to read.

Text-only pages are fast to load, but can be a bit boring. Colour adds impact to your screens, without adding to the loading time.

```
<HTML>
<HEAD>
<TITLE>Colours</TITLE>
</HEAD>

<BODY BGCOLOR = "white" TEXT = "navy blue">
<H1>Colours</H1>
<H2>
<FONT COLOR = red> Changing to red <BR>
<FONT COLOR = orange> Changing to orange <BR>
<FONT COLOR = yellow> Changing to yellow <BR>
<FONT COLOR = green> Changing to green <BR>
<FONT COLOR = blue> Changing to blue <BR>
<FONT COLOR = maroon> Changing to maroon <BR>
<FONT COLOR = fuchsia> Changing to fuchsia <BR>
</FONT> and back to maroon <BR>
</FONT> and back to blue
</H2>
</BODY>
</HTML>
```

1 Start a new file in your editor.

2 Type in the sample text shown opposite, varying colours as you like.

3 Save the file as 'colours.htm'.

4 Open the file in Internet Explorer to see how it looks.

Important

!

Note the US spelling COLOR – COLOUR will not work!

Setting the text size

The <FONT> tag can take a number of other options as well as COLOR, and one which you really should know about is SIZE. This option takes a value between 1 and 7 and sets the size of the text as follows: 1 = 8 point, 2 = 10 point, 3 = 12 point, 4 = 14 point, 5 = 18 point, 6 = 24 point, 7 = 36 point.

1 Start a new file in your editor.

2 Type in the code shown here, using your own words for font size samples.

3 Save the file as fontsize.htm.

4 Open the file in Internet Explorer to see how it looks.

```
<HTML>
<HEAD>
<TITLE>Font Size</TITLE>
</HEAD>
<BODY>
<H1>Font Size</H1>
<FONT SIZE = 1>This is font size 1</FONT><BR>
<FONT SIZE = 2>This is font size 2</FONT><BR>
<FONT SIZE = 3>This is font size 3</FONT><BR>
<FONT SIZE = 4>This is font size 4</FONT><BR>
<FONT SIZE = 5>This is font size 5</FONT><BR>
<FONT SIZE = 6>This is font size 6</FONT><BR>
<FONT SIZE = 7>This is font size 7</FONT><BR>
</BODY>
</HTML>
```

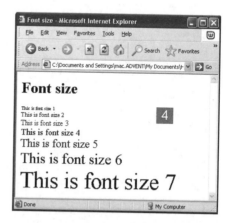

You can use this at the start to set the size of the text for the whole page, or at any point within it. You can even vary the size within paragraphs, to make words really stand out, or for special effects.

Lines, or Horizontal Rules, are created with the tag <HR>. This is a single tag – there is no </HR> to end it. A simple <HR> produces a thin 3D-effect line.

For variety, use the options:

SIZE to set the thickness. This is measured in pixels, e.g.

<HR SIZE = 6>

WIDTH can also be set in pixels or as a percentage of the width of the browser window, e.g.

<HR WIDTH = 100>

<HR SIZE = 6 WIDTH = 50%>

NOSHADE makes the line solid, e.g.

<HR SIZE = 6 WIDTH = 250 NOSHADE>

```
<HTML>
<HEAD>
<TITLE>Lines</TITLE>
</HEAD>
<BODY>
<H1>Lines</H1>
The basic tag draws this simple line.
<HR>
You can set its thickness with the size option
<HR SIZE = 10>
You can make it solid with 'noshade'
<HR SIZE = 10 NOSHADE>
And set its width as a percentage of the window...
<HR WIDTH = 60%>
...or give the width in pixels
<HR WIDTH = 150>
</BODY>
</HMTL>
```

Drawing a line

1

1 Start a new file in your editor.

2 Type in this sample text, varying the SIZE, WIDTH and NOSHADE options as you like.

3 Save the file as 'lines.htm'.

4 Open the file in Internet Explorer to see how it looks.

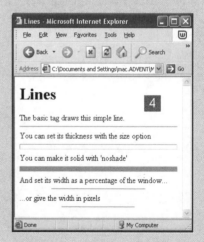

Making a list

There are two types of lists. Both are constructed in the same way.

- <OL> </OL> (ordered/numbered) or <UL> </UL> (unordered/bulleted) enclose the whole list.

- Each item in the list is enclosed by <LI> </LI> tags, e.g.

    <UL>

        <LI>List item</LI>

        <LI>List item</LI>

    </UL>

Bullets are normally round. You can set the style to SQUARE with the TYPE option, e.g.

    <UL TYPE = SQUARE>

1. Start a new file in your editor.

2. Type in this sample code, varying the text.

3. Save the file as 'lists.htm'.

4. Open the file in Internet Explorer to see how it looks.

5. Edit the code to produce square bullets. Change the <UL> tag to read:
<UL TYPE = SQUARE>.

6. Save the file and reload it into the browser to see the effect.

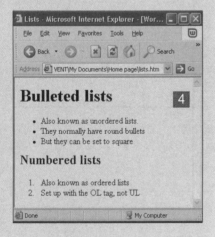

```
<HTML>
<HEAD>
<TITLE>Lists</TITLE>
</HEAD>
<BODY>
<H1>Bulleted lists</H1>
<UL>
<LI>Also known as unordered lists.</LI>
<LI>They normally have round bullets</LI>
<LI>But they can be set to square</LI>
</UL>
<H2>Numbered lists</H2>
<OL>
<LI>Also known as ordered lists</LI>
<LI>Set up with the OL tag, not UL</LI>
</OL>
</BODY>
</HTML>
```

Hyperlinks are the most important aspect of hypertext – without them, the web simply wouldn't exist. There are two parts to a hyperlink – it must define the page or file that is being linked, and mark the text or image that will be clicked to activate the jump. The basic shape is:

<A HREF=*where_to_link*> *clickable_object*</A>

The clickable_object can be a word or phrase – by itself or embedded in other text – or an image. Hyperlinked text is usually coloured and underlined, and images are normally outlined. Here we are using text – we'll add hyperlinks to images on pages 20–22 and 134.

```
<HTML>
<HEAD>
<TITLE>Links</TITLE>
</HEAD>
<BODY>
<H1>Hypertext links</H1>
<A HREF = http://www.google.co.uk> Go to Google </A>
<P>
<A HREF = http://www.bbc.co.uk/home/today> BBC online
</A>
<P> <A HREF = index.htm> Back to home page at this site
</A>
</BODY>
</HTML>
```

where_to_link can be the name of another page on your site:

<A HREF="products.htm"> Product list </A>

or the URL of a page somewhere else on the web:

<A HREF="http://www.yahoo.co.uk"> Go to Yahoo! </A>

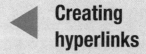

Creating hyperlinks

1 Start a new file in your editor.

2 Type in this sample code, using your own choice of web addresses.

3 Save the file as 'links.htm'.

Creating hyperlinks (cont.)

4. Open the file in Internet Explorer to see how it looks.

5. Go online, if necessary, and click on the links to check that they work. (And come straight back once you reach a site – the aim is to test the links, not to go surfing!).

Jargon buster

Hyperlinks – connections between different web pages and websites made possible using URLs.

Hypertext – a dynamic form of cross-referencing that is used in web pages to allow the reader to simply 'click' through to the referenced document or file rather than having to look it up manually.

Did you know?

Hyperlinks can also link to other parts of the same page, so that you can move around a long document, or to a video or other file, or to an email address.

To display an image on a web page it must be in the right format. Browsers can only handle JPEG and GIF images.

See also

See pages 88 and 89 for more information on file formats.

Jargon buster

JPEG – short for Joint Photographic Experts Group – the committee that developed the file format. It specifies the way that colours are transformed into bytes and is ideal for photographs and other continuous colour images.

GIF files – short for Graphics Interchange Format – graphics files that use a palette of up to 256 distinct colours to produce an image. This makes them ideal for images which use solid blocks of colour but unsuitable for colour photographs or images that use continuous colour.

You can specify the size of an image in the browser, whatever its real size, e.g. you could set a 1,200 by 800 image to be displayed at 300 by 200 pixels. You can also set it to be a certain percentage of the window size, so that it always occupies the same relative amount of space,

whatever the size of the page. The actual size of the image should not be more than the maximum size at which it is displayed. Images add to the download time, especially for those on dial-up connections, and over-large images slow things down needlessly.

See also

See pages 108–118 for more information on compressing your images and optimising download times.

To get your images into the right size and the right format, you will need some form of image processing software. If you have a digital camera, it probably came with some suitable software. If not, there are plenty of good shareware graphics programs out there. All you need is something that can handle different file formats, including JPEG and GIF, and that can resize images.

The basic image tag is:

    <IMG SRC = 'filename'>

You can also use these options:

    ALIGN = 'left/center/right'

    ALT = 'description'

    WIDTH = value

    HEIGHT = value

Understanding the basics of displaying images (cont.)

ALIGN sets the position of the image across the page. Note the US spelling 'center'. The UK spelling 'centre' will not work!

ALT is the text to display if the image is not loaded into a browser, and also the tip that will appear if you hover the mouse over the image. In the example in the next task, if image loading was turned off, you would see this:

☒ View from a nearby window

WIDTH and HEIGHT set the size of the image in the page. You can set the size as a percentage of either the width or height, or set it in pixels, giving both the width and the height.

```
<IMG SRC = 'tiddles.jpg' ALT = 'this is my cat'
WIDTH = 80%>
```

This will display the picture of Tiddles, shrinking – or expanding – the image size so that it fills 80% of the width of the browser window.

Did you know?

If you set the image width to 100%, it will be resized to fit the browser window, whatever size it may be.

Jargon buster

ALT tags – textual descriptions of web page elements, such as images and icons, that appear when the user's mouse hovers over the element.

```
<HTML>
<HEAD>
<TITLE>Images</TITLE>
</HEAD>

<BODY>
<H3>The Church at La Reole</H3>
<IMG SRC = "church1.jpg" ALT = "View from a nearby
window">
<BR>
<ADDRESS>September 2004</ADDRESS>
</BODY>
</HTML>
```

1. Find or prepare a suitable image to use on your web page.
2. Start a new file in your editor.
3. Create a page along the lines shown opposite, using your file and with suitable heading and ALT text.
4. Save the file as 'images.htm'.
5. Open the file in Internet Explorer. How does it look? What happens if you change the size of the Internet Explorer window?
6. Edit the code to set the image at 80% of the screen width. You will need to add this in the <IMG SRC...> tag: WIDTH = 80%.
7. Save the file and reload it into the browser to see the effect.

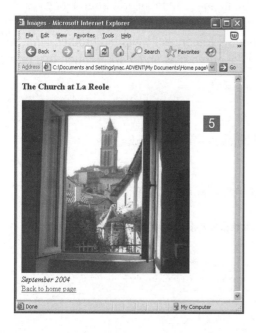

Important

! If you are putting photos on the web so that other people can print them out, then they should be left at their original size for best printed results. Longer download time will just be the price to pay.

Linking a thumbnail to an image

Create the image pages

1 Take the first image file. If you want to reduce download time, resize it to fit neatly onto the screen.

2 Save the file with a name that will remind you of its content.

3 Re-size the image again, reducing it to a thumbnail of 100-200 pixels width. Save this with a name that is based on the full-size image – add 'thumb' or 'mini' or a number to the end.

4 Go to your editor and start a new HTML file.

5 There are only two essential lines in the BODY area: an <IMG SRC...> tag to display the image, and a hyperlink to jump back to the thumbnails page. This doesn't exist yet, but we can still write the tag <A HREF = thumbnails.htm>.

If you have a set of large photos that you want to share with your friends and family, you could do this by emailing copies of all of them to all of your circle. This may not always be welcome. Even on broadband, it could take a while for a lot of emails with attached images to download, and it could lock up a slow dial-up connection for hours. Here's a better way.

If you place your photos on your website, and tell your friends about them, they can visit in their own time. And if you organise the photos so that visitors can view and select from 'thumbnails', then they will only have to wait to see the images that they really want. To set this up, you would need to take each of the photos into your graphics software, resize it down to 150 or so pixels wide or high, and save it with a new name. Each full-size image is then inserted into its own web page. All the thumbnails are added to a single page, and each one will have a hyperlink to connect to its big brother. Find two or three suitable digital photo files and work through this next exercise.

```
<HTML>
<HEAD>
<TITLE>Photos: the canal</TITLE>
</HEAD>
<BODY>
<IMG SRC = "canal.jpg" WIDTH = 100%>
<BR>
<A HREF = thumbnails.htm> Back to thumbnails</A>
</BODY>
</HTML>
```

6 Save the page file with the same name as the image file.

7 Repeat steps 1 to 6 for the other images.

8 View the file in Internet Explorer.

Create the thumbnail page

1 Start a new HTML file.

2 Type in code along the lines shown here, changing the title, heading and filenames to suit your pages and images, and adding suitable ALT text to the images.

```
<HTML>
<HEAD>
<TITLE>My holiday snaps</TITLE>
</HEAD>
<BODY>
<H2>Photos from my French holiday</H2>
<A HREF = vines.htm> <IMG SRC = "vinesmini.jpg" ALT =
"Vines near the Dropt"> </A>
<A HREF = church.htm> <IMG SRC = "churchmini.jpg" ALT =
"The Church at La Reole"> </A>
<A HREF = canal.htm> <IMG SRC = "canalmini.jpg" ALT = "The
Canal Lateral"> </A>
<BR>
</BODY>
</HTML>
```

Important

Notice how the <IMG SRC…> tags fit between the <A HREF…> and </A> tags.

Linking a thumbnail to an image (cont.)

3 Save it as 'thumbnails.htm'.

4 Open the thumbnails file in Internet Explorer.

5 Click on a thumbnail and you should jump to the page with its full-size image.

6 Click the Back to thumbnails link to return to the thumbnails page.

7 Follow the links to the other images.

If you have worked through the examples so far, you should now have a dozen or so web page files. What we now need to do is link them together to turn them into a site. To do this, we will edit the index.htm file – our Welcome page – and write into it hyperlinks to the other pages. We then edit each of the second-level pages in turn, adding a hyperlink to take visitors back to the top page.

```
<HTML>
<HEAD>
<TITLE>Mac's web site at Wanadoo</TITLE>
</HEAD>
<BODY>
<H1>Welcome to my site</H1>
<FONT SIZE = 5>
<A HREF = text.htm> Formatting text </A> <BR>
<A HREF = colours.htm> Colours </A> <BR>
<A HREF = fontsize.htm> Font size </A> <BR>
<A HREF = lines.htm> Lines </A> <BR>
<A HREF = lists.htm> Lists </A> <BR>
<A HREF = links.htm> Links </A> <BR>
<A HREF = images.htm> Images </A> <BR>
<A HREF = thumbnails.htm> Linked images </A> <BR>
</FONT>
</BODY>
</HTML>
```

Linking pages in a website

1

1. Open the index.htm file in your editor.

2. Edit the file to add hyperlinks to each of the second-level pages.

3. Save the file.

4. Open the first of the other pages and add this line at the bottom of the code, just before the </BODY> tag:

    <A HREF = index.htm> Back to home page</A>

5. Save the file.

6. Repeat for the rest of the pages.

7. Open the index.htm file in Internet Explorer.

8. Use the links to open the other pages in turn, going back to the index each time.

Jargon buster

Web page – a document accessed using a web browser. It may be plain or formatted text and may hold pictures, sound files and videos.

Creating a web page in Word

1 Open Word.

2 If the New Document task pane is not visible, open the File menu and select New...

3 Select Blank Web Page from the New options.

4 Open the File menu and select Save as Web Page...

You can produce web pages in Word – and you don't have to think about which tags to use. You write and format the page more or less as you would any other Word document, using the normal tools. The only difference is that you save it in web page file format. Word replaces its own formatting and layout codes with HTML tags, and outputs a standard HTML text file.

Note the 'more or less' back there. Web pages are different from documents produced for printing, and this has a little impact on the way that you work in Word. The first thing to note is that web pages are not a fixed shape – they are not A4!

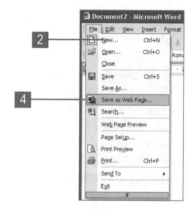

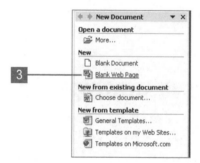

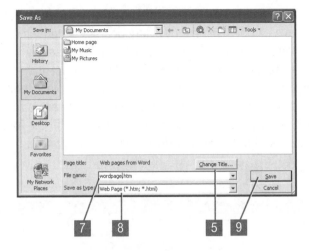

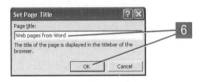

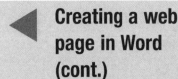
5 If there is a heading in the page, this will be offered as the Page Title. If not, or if you don't want the suggested title, click Change Title…

6 Enter the title and click OK.

7 Edit the suggested File name or enter a new one.

8 Check that the Save as type field is set to Web Page.

9 Click Save.

Important

!

When you are creating any document – not just web pages – it is good practice to save a file immediately, even though it is still blank. This sets the file name and the file format. While you are working on it, you should resave regularly – and all you need to do then is click the Save button.

Formatting text in Word

HTML formatting is more limited than normal Word formatting. Most tools can be used happily, although some options can raise problems. Fonts are best left alone. If you use any other than the standard ones – Times New Roman, Arial and Wingdings – there's no guarantee that other people will have them on their PC, so your page may not look the same to them. Similarly, borders, highlights and changes in the font size, may not be displayed properly on some browsers.

1 Type your text as normal. When formatting, use:

- Styles for headings;

- Bold and Italic for emphasis;

- Left, Right and Centre buttons to set alignment;

- Numbered and bulleted lists buttons to create UL and OL lists;

- Text colour button.

2 Save regularly.

3 Open the file in Internet Explorer to check its appearance. It should look very similar to how it is in Word.

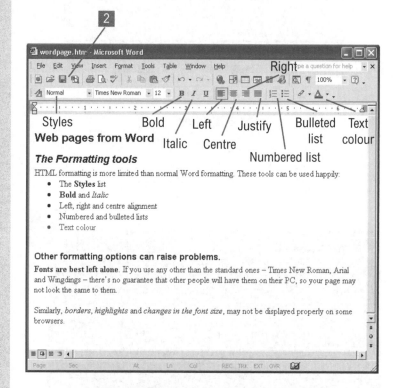

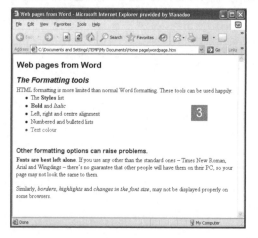

Word has a simple routine for creating hyperlinks, though it has one little oddity that you must be aware of. When you write the address into the dialog box, if it doesn't start with 'www...' you must type 'http://' before the address. For example, to link to the main BBC site you could use www.bbc.co.uk, but to link to the News site you would have to write http://news.bbc.co.uk

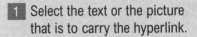

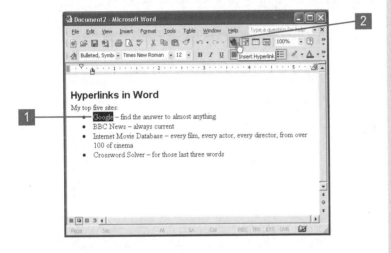

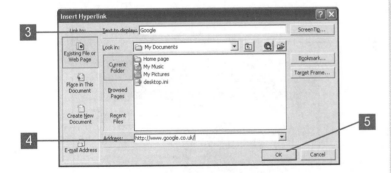

◀ **Creating a link in Word**

1

1 Select the text or the picture that is to carry the hyperlink.

2 Click on the Insert Hyperlink button.

3 At the Insert Hyperlink dialog box, check that the Text to display is correct.

4 Type in the Address, preceded by 'http://' if it doesn't start with 'www'.

5 Click OK.

Did you know?

Hyperlinks can be written into any kind of Word document – not just web pages.

Following links in Word

As well as creating hyperlinks in Word, you can also start browsing from them, and although you are no longer in Word when you do that, Windows software is so integrated that you will switch to Internet Explorer in the same window and may not even notice it! Simply clicking or double-clicking on a hyperlink in Word does no more than if it were plain text. But if you hold down [Ctrl], a click will activate the link.

1 Go online if you are not already connected.

2 Hold down [Ctrl].

3 Point to the text of image carrying the link – a tip box will appear showing the linked address.

4 Click to go. The Word window will become an Internet Explorer window, and the linked page will be displayed.

5 Click on Back to return to your original page in Word.

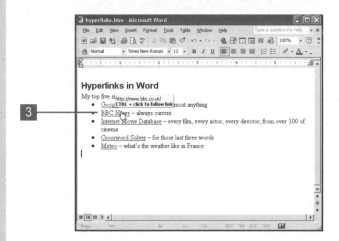

Researching and planning your first website

Introduction

Before you start on your first project it's a good idea to decide what sort of website you want to build. Think about the sort of pages that you're interested in and what you yourself look out for when surfing the web. You'll save lots of time during the building process if you have a clear idea of the direction you want to take your project in. Having said that, the beauty of websites is that, unlike a printed project, you can update or change anything you like either as you go along or after completion. During the course of this chapter we'll be looking at the various types of website that can be produced by a beginner and then providing some advice on planning and managing your website files.

What you'll do

Research personal websites

Take a look at hobbyist and club websites

Consider a small business website

Plan your project on paper

Manage your files

Find online resources: content

Final thoughts on planning a website

Researching personal websites

If you're a bona fide beginner and want to start exploring the world of web page construction, then perhaps one of the easiest places to start is to create a personal website. This is a great way to discover what lies behind the art of page design and can be a great deal of fun too. Even better is the fact that all of the material you'll want to put on the site can be easily sourced without you having to go to too much trouble.

1 A good place to start browsing through personal web pages is at: http://geocities.yahoo.com/. Click browse.

2 Every directory of websites contains so many they have to be categorised by topic area. We have selected Family and Home to focus on personal sites.

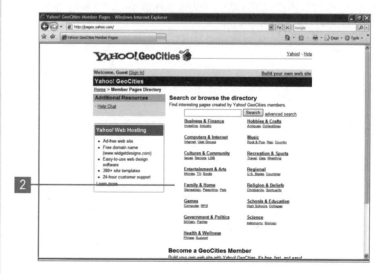

3 Select Families, General to be presented with over 9,000 sites to browse!

4 Continue browsing in the other categories and you'll soon see that people use websites to express all kinds of views, from trivia through to serious issues.

Important

You should bear in mind that all ISPs will vet the content of your web page projects so don't consider producing anything that features questionable content. Be respectful to your fellow web users at all times.

Taking a look at hobbyist and club websites

If you're passionate about a particular hobby or pastime then starting a club and creating a web page for it is the perfect way to use the power of the internet. By posting your page on the web you'll be able to share ideas and thoughts with others who have the same interests. Hobbyist or club websites come in all shapes and sizes and inspiration for this sort of website design can be found all over the internet. The major web portals, such as Yahoo, are perhaps the best places to start your search.

1. To start your club site research, go to http://uk.yahoo.com. Scroll down to the bottom of the page and click on More Web Directories.

2. This is the Directory Home page and it contains a collection of links to the most popular topics. Click on the Hobbies link under Recreation & Sport.

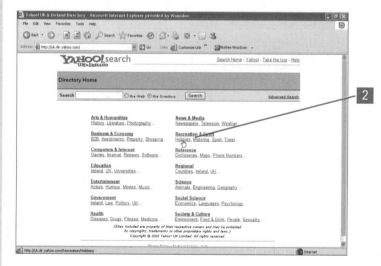

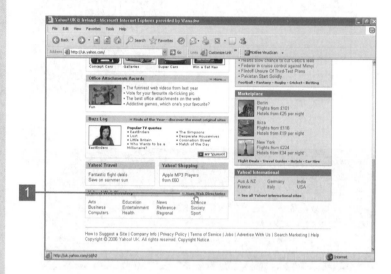

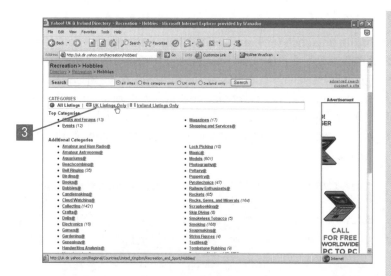

3 A cornucopia of websites is unveiled! Built by amateurs and professionals alike, there are plenty to browse and glean ideas from. You can also pick UK only listings if you wish.

2

For your information

We've used Yahoo here but you can find the same sort of information on any of the other major web portals such as AOL, MSN, Virgin, etc.

Did you know?

Related websites can be interlinked to form a Webring so that visitors can visit each site in turn and eventually return to the first. The ring is managed by one 'hub' site that allows visitors to navigate their way through the ring either sequentially or randomly.

Jargon buster

Webring – a community of similarly themed websites that are linked so that users can navigate their way through them via a single 'hub'.

Jargon buster

Web portal – a gateway or entrance to a selection of websites that may be categorised to help the user find sites he/she is interested in. Additional features are often added to encourage web users to use a specific portal as their default starting site when browsing, such as news feeds, search engine facilities and personalisation options.

Considering a small business website

More and more people are realising the benefit of creating an online presence for their business, be it a part-time hobby or full-time job. Remember, this doesn't necessarily mean that you will be selling goods over the internet. You can build a simple site that you can point customers at for information and to promote what you do. At the same time though, there is untold scope for anyone who wants to start selling products via the web.

1 We'll use the Yahoo Directory again and select Business & Economy, Business to Business. Choose a category that reflects your business interests and browse some sites to get an idea of what the competition is up to.

2 Alternatively, try this list of the Best of the Best Business websites – all American but design is universal!

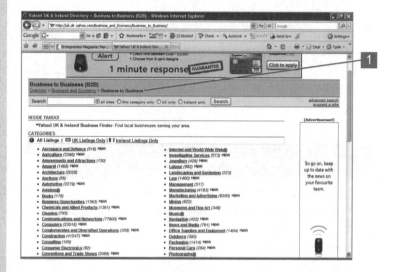

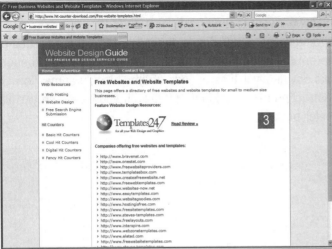

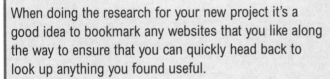

2

3 There's plenty of help for anybody looking to start their own business on the web and remember that it is amazingly cheap and easy to set up a functioning website on your own, so don't jump into signing up to a professional service until you have checked out the plentiful free options available.

Timesaver tip

When doing the research for your new project it's a good idea to bookmark any websites that you like along the way to ensure that you can quickly head back to look up anything you found useful.

Jargon buster

Bookmark – a way of keeping a record of websites that you want to visit again. Your browser keeps a list of the URLs as 'your favourites' so you can easily return to them without having to remember the web addresses.

Planning your project on paper

Now that you've spent some time researching the type of project you want to undertake, it's a good time to start mapping it out. A few simple diagrams are all that's needed to map out the basic format and structure of your site. Although it looks obvious, you'll save loads of time when it comes to constructing the actual files and links if you have a proper plan to refer back to.

1 Sketch out the details of your first web page. Annotate it with formatting and design features you've seen in the sites you like.

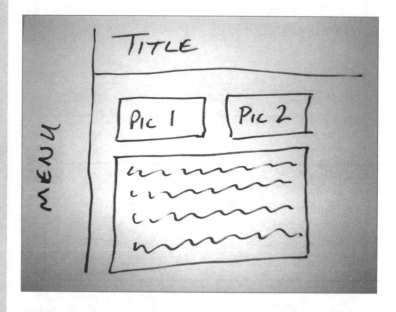

For your information

The engineers who produce the superb website authoring package, Macromedia Dreamweaver, have some great tips on creating goals for your site, organising the structure, creating your design 'look' and more at www.macromedia.com/support/dreamweaver/layout/site_planning. And Sucky to Savvy at http://jeffglover.com/ss.php offers some excellent planning tips and highlights common mistakes and design no-no's.

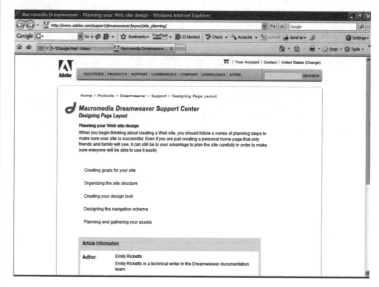

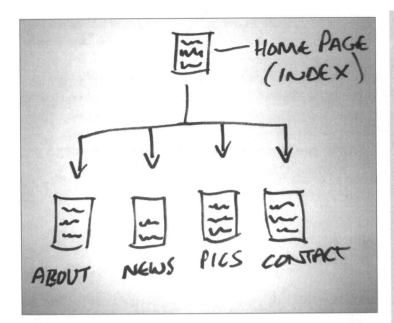

2 If the website will consist of more than one page, always start out with the home page and then add subsequent pages in a hierarchical manner. Use arrows to indicate how the pages link to each other.

2

See also

Our section on web usability design tips in Chapter 7, pages 162–167 provides some very helpful advice on how to make your site as user-friendly as possible.

For your information

The top or home page is normally called 'index.htm', although this is not needed in the address. When you type 'www.mysite.com' into the browser, it actually looks for 'www.mysite.com/index.htm'. Every other page in your site will radiate out from this.

Managing your files

Having a traditional plan or map of all the content and pages that you wish to include in your website will make it much easier to create electronic versions of the same thing once you start putting your HTML files together. It is vital to store and manage your files systematically as anything filed in the wrong place will result in broken links and missing content when your site goes live.

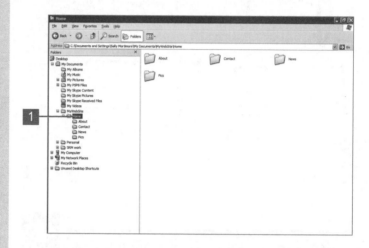

1 First of all, create a dedicated website folder and arrange sub-folders hierarchically, mirroring your paper plan.

2 Store all your files, graphics and text, in the appropriate sub-folders of your root directory so you can keep track of what you need for each page of your site.

Important

Be aware that software applications often save new files by default in a folder within the program file. For example, CoffeeCup creates a 'Working' folder and automatically puts newly created files in there. You can easily redirect them to your Root folder – you just need to remember to do it.

Important

The main folder, which is used to keep web page content along with images and any other site building essentials, is known as the 'Root'. Be sure to store everything inside this dedicated folder.

The content you chose for your site will help to entice visitors and give them some reason to come back. Incorporate these ideas into your plan if you think they are appropriate.

If you want news feeds for your website, offering the latest headline from various news sites, try the link at www.easybyte.com/products/. Offering this kind of service to visitors can hardly fail to impress.

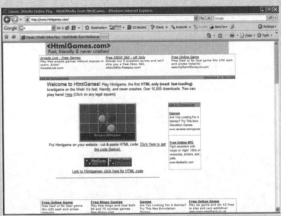

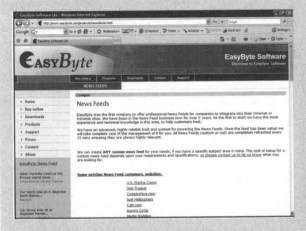

The free information at http://fantomaster.com/faarticles0.html will be of special interest to webmasters – you can copy and paste the articles into your own website for free.

If yours is the kind of site where free games would be appropriate and welcomed, try the offerings at www.groovynet.com/javagames. Also useful is www.htmlgames.com which offers a variation of the classic game Othello.

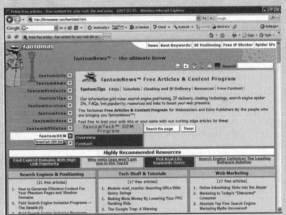

Finding online resources: content (cont.)

How about some free recipes for your visitors? The popularity of cookery in general should mean that this will prove to be a popular addition to your site. Try www.wwrecipes.com/link.htm to see what you need to do.

Wordsmiths will also be in heaven if you offer a 'word of the day' service – try http://dictionary. reference.com/help/linking/wordoftheday.html for the lowdown on what to do.

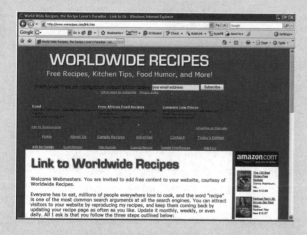

Final thoughts on planning a website

The hardest parts of creating a website are deciding what to publish and how to present it. Compared with these, the mechanics of putting pages together are quite simple!

- Who are the pages for? Friends and family, fellow fans, others with shared interests or potential customers? The more you are trying to attract new people to your site, the more care you must take over its design.

- If a page is mainly text, can it be conveniently broken up into screen-sized chunks? People do not like scrolling through long pages to get to the bit that interests them. On the other hand, if it is continuous text – a story or article – then it is better to present it on one long page. This makes it easier for your visitors to save it for reading offline later.

- Images add to the attractiveness of pages, but they add to download time. Think about why and how you use them.

- Your web pages will be viewed in different sizes of windows. Screens range from 1920×1200 to 640×480 pixels, and people may not run their browsers at full screen. A page which looks good on your big screen, may not work in a small window.

- Aim for a clean, unfussy design, with a good contrast between the text and background colours, and readable-sized text, with headings that are large enough to be noticeable without dominating the screen.

- How will you structure your material? You shouldn't try to put too much on a single page, so for anything other than the simplest page, you must think about how it can be organised.

2

Creating a website using online services

Introduction

Perhaps one of the quickest, cheapest and low-maintenance ways of creating a website in simple steps is to build one without having to purchase any kind of software at all, using one of the many different services available on the Internet. This chapter will take you through the steps involved in creating a website online – a useful exercise in itself as it allows you to gain an understanding of website design without requiring any financial outlay. We will also demonstrate how to create a web blog – a dynamic diary style website that allows readers to respond with their own comments, and touch briefly on some of the less formal individual home pages being created in their thousands on MySpaces.

Jargon buster

Web blog – an interactive online journal or diary or commentary on events and issues where content is provided both by the originator and the readers in the form of comments.

Personal home page – a web page focusing on an individual and his/her interests.

What you'll do

Pick an online web page creation service

Construct a web page using the free Zyweb trial

Customise your web page

Publish a web page

Create a site with WebEden

Customise a WebEden site

Get your pages online

Make your own web blog

Update your blog

Create a MySpace personal home page

Picking an online web page creation service ▶

When it comes to creating a website using an online service there are plenty to choose from. Much of the hard coding work is done 'behind the scenes' for you and there's certainly very little technical knowledge needed, although some of the more advanced packages do allow you to tinker around with the page designs and coding if you wish to customise the way your web pages look. You'll find that different services charge different fees for what they offer. Many are free but the more sophisticated services charge a monthly fee or subscription.

1 A simple search on Google illustrates the dazzling array of services available. It is worth exploring the features of the individual packages. Some offer all manner of bells and whistles, others are frill-free. Explore the different services to find the one that best suits your needs.

2 We have chosen to use ZyWeb, located at www.zyweb.com, which enables you to build a complete website in minutes.

3 You can take a guided tour of the features that are on offer. Go to their home page and click on the link that says 'Watch our movies to see how easy it is'. A selection of movies show how to create a master page, store files, insert audio and video, etc.

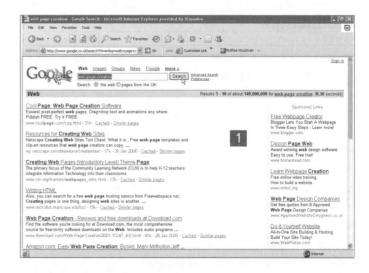

For your information

Don't worry if you don't have the software to view the movie files. There is a link on the web page that will take you to the Microsoft website where the Windows Media Player can be downloaded for free.

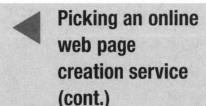

4 Chose which of the different packages best suits your needs: Business (comes with a free domain name), Personal or TimeSaver (the site will be built for you).

5 It's a good idea to read up on the details of the individual packages before opting to 'buy now'.

3

Timesaver tip

You really need a broadband internet connection if you are going to use an online service. Creating web pages with a dial-up connection is possible, but very time consuming. If you only have access to a dial-up connection, consider building your website on your computer (see Chapters 1, 4 and 6) and see page 184 for details on how to upload your files to the internet.

Constructing a web page using the free ZyWeb trial

One of the best things about many of the online web page creation services is that you can use them for a trial period without paying anything at all. In the case of ZyWeb, you will have around a month to explore the package features which include an automated page builder system, a web graphics toolkit, photo editor and tools for promoting your pages once you've designed and built them. You'll need to upgrade (and therefore pay!) in order to save your website, but the trial does let you get plenty of construction practice first.

1 It only takes a few minutes to register with the service.

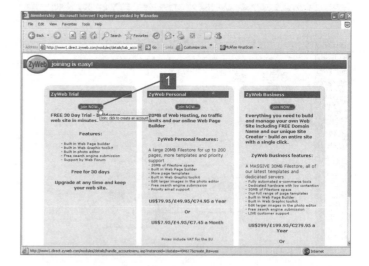

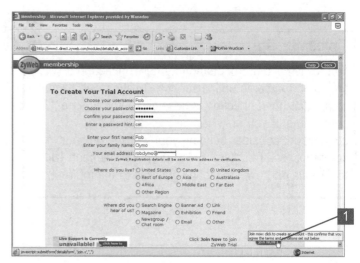

Constructing a web page using the free ZyWeb trial (cont.)

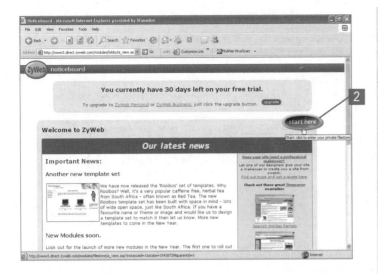

2 Now you'll be directed to the start of your ZyWeb trial period. You can spend a little time getting acquainted with the features or simply click on 'start here'.

3 The design area is very simple and straightforward. All of the options needed to complete the job are found in the left-hand menu. Click on Web Page to create your first document.

3

For your information

Note the Help button in the toolbar at the top right-hand side of the window.

Constructing a web page using the free ZyWeb trial (cont.)

4 Select a style – scroll down, there are plenty to chose from. ZyWeb, and the other online services like it, work by having a series of pre-designed web page templates that you simply select and then customise for your own unique project.

5 We will select this clean, simple page style for a personal home page project.

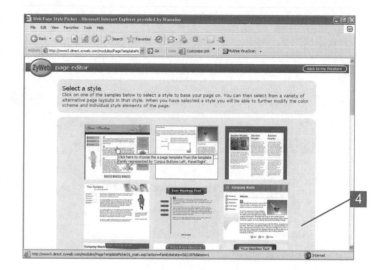

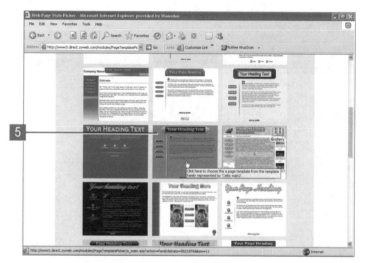

Jargon buster

Web page template – a pre-designed web page layout that can be adapted or customised for a particular use.

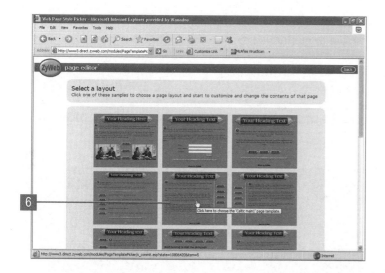

Constructing a web page using the free ZyWeb trial (cont.)

6 Select a layout. This gives you the opportunity to select a layout that suits the content of your page – be it mostly text, pictures or links to other pages.

3

For your information

You can take a break from ZyWeb at any time, but if you leave the site you'll need your Login name and password to get back to your project.

Customising your web page

You can now edit each of the elements in the web page template to customise it.

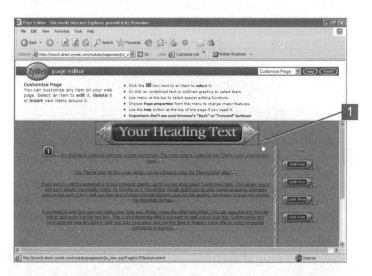

1. When you click on any of the Edit tabs on your page, the tab becomes active and a toolbar appears at the top of the ZyWeb window. This is where you can carry out the editing process.

2. Simply type your new text, e.g. 'My Web Page' into the text field as shown. If you're happy with the way it looks then all you need to do is click OK.

3. Alternatively, explore your options for changing styles, size and quality as well as turning the heading into a link to another page.

4. Add your own text. Click on the Edit tab by the paragraph discussing text. As soon as you select this option the toolbar at the top of the screen becomes a text editor.

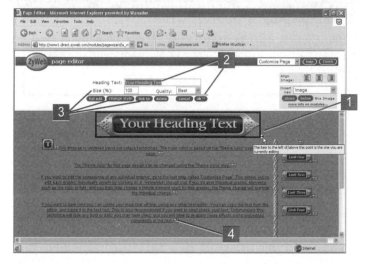

For your information

There are more powerful tool options within ZyWeb and these can be explored by clicking on the Full Edit button but if you're still finding your way around then stick to the default settings for now.

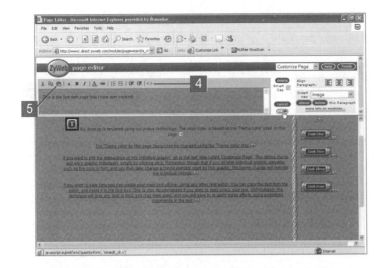

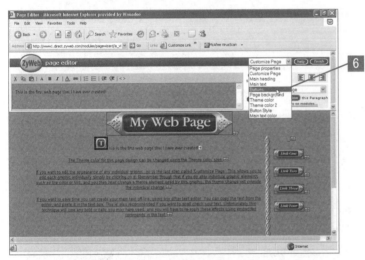

You'll probably want to customise your page even more by tinkering with the design. You can control all of this creative work using the drop-down menu located at the top right-hand side of your screen.

5 The options for formatting your text should be familiar. You can use the Copy and Paste functions to copy text from other documents stored on your computer so that you don't have to type it all in manually.

6 The drop-down menu allows you to edit the style or design of many additional web page elements – buttons, headings, background colour, text colour, etc. Simply select an element and editing options will be displayed in the page editor. The Page properties tool allows you to adapt the theme you have chosen, copy a theme from another page, and add features such as a visitor counter and feedback form.

3

Jargon buster

URL – Uniform Resource Locator – a standard way to identify the location of web pages and other documents that can be accessed via the web.

Customising your web page (cont.)

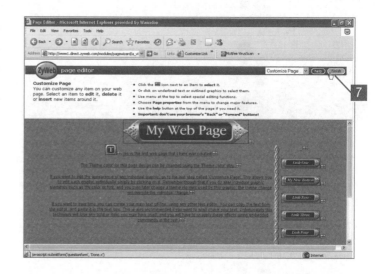

7 Once you are happy with your web page, click Finish.

8 Save your web pages as you create them, amending file name and page category as necessary.

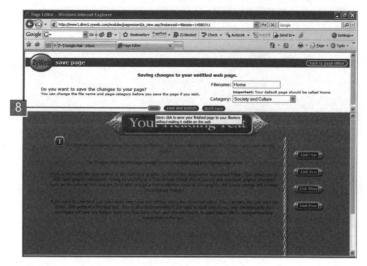

Important

Clearly, buttons need to link to another web page or website. When you create buttons you are given the option of linking them to a URL or to another of your own web pages. Editing this element is therefore perhaps left until you have created all the web pages you plan to include in your website.

As you are using an online subscription service, publishing your website is the matter of a couple of clicks. Your files will be stored on ZyWeb's server and made available via their domain name: www.zyworld.com.

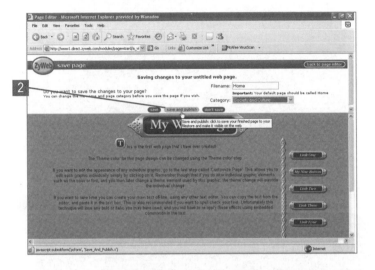

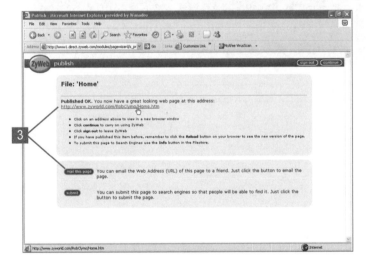

1 If everything looks just as it should, go to the top right hand corner of the browser window and click Finish.

2 Click on Save and publish and you're done.

3 It's a good idea to make a note of the link to your web page so that you can pass it onto others. Better still, click on the 'Mail this page' link on the ZyWeb page to send it directly to family, friends and anyone else you want to show it to.

3

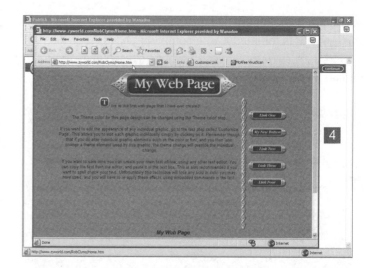

4 Here is the page we have just created and it is live and on the web. Now that you know the basics, you can log back into the ZyWeb service and start making the additional necessary changes to the page.

Important

Remember that the ZyWeb creation system requires you to be connected to the Internet. So, ensure that you have a permanent connection and avoid clicking your web browser's Back or Forward buttons whilst working.

Now that you've seen just how easy it is to create a web page using the online services of ZyWeb, we'll explore another option. WebEden is a similar service to ZyWeb but despite the simplicity of its features, WebEden is surprisingly powerful and comes armed with a dazzling array of easy-to-use options for producing stylish web pages. What's more, if you go to www.webeden.co.uk you'll find that it offers a free 14 day trial which you can use to explore all of the features on offer.

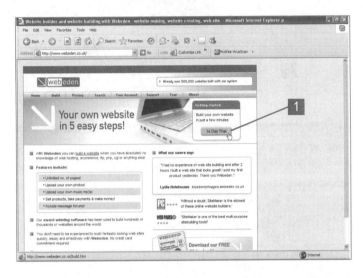

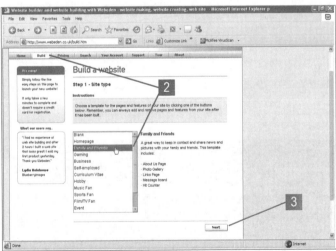

1 Go to the WebEden home page at www.webeden.co.uk to get started and click on the 14 Day Trial button on the right-hand side of the screen.

2 Click on the Build tab to start. Select a site type that suits your purposes from the templates available – take note of the descriptions that pop up to the right of the menu. Remember that you can edit and customise the format further so don't be put off if you can't find the perfect match at this stage.

3 Click on Next to continue.

Important

Whilst the WebEden 14 day trial is free, you'll need to pay to keep your site online. Click on the Pricing tab to find details of the various packages – there are a host of different options ranging from a few pounds a month for a very basic service through to pricier packages aimed at more advanced users.

Creating a site with WebEden (cont.)

4 Select a design style and colour – again remembering that you can edit the settings later if required. Click on each of the menu options to preview the options. You can use the small Choose a colour button on the right to transform the design still further.

5 Click Next.

6 The third step in the process requires you to enter a unique website address so that you and others can access the site you create. Also type in a name for the website logo beneath this and click Next.

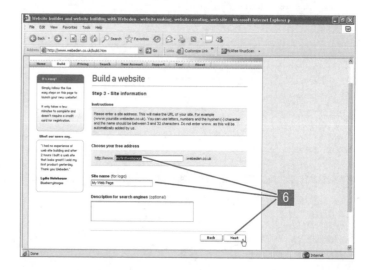

For your information

Notice that WebEden will automatically add a webeden.co.uk extension to your website name.

Important

It's worth spending some time trying all of the different colour schemes to see which one suits you the most, but bear in mind that it is easy to come back to any step of the process later on and, with a click of your mouse, transform the design of your web pages.

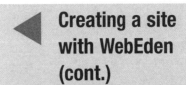

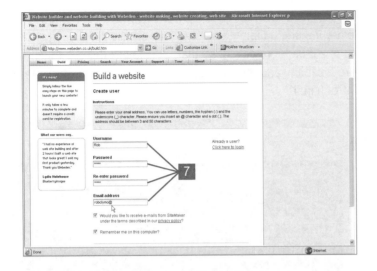

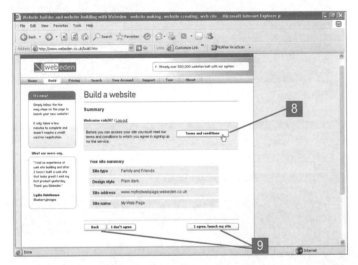

7 Finally, you'll need to create your user account by supplying the necessary details. You should type in a user name, password and then a confirmation of the password along with a valid email address. You'll need to know these details in order to Log into and out of the WebEden service in future.

8 The WebEden service requires that you read their terms and conditions before you progress any further. Once done, simply use the Back button to return to the site summary page.

9 If you're happy with the choices you've made, click on I agree, launch my site. If not, there's a Back button to allow you to make changes.

3

! Important

There are two check boxes at the bottom of this window. The top one, if checked, means you will automatically receive product information from the WebEden SiteMaker service. The bottom one enables your own computer to remember your login details so you don't have to type them in each time you re-enter the site.

Customising a
WebEden site

With an account set up and ready to run you're now able to explore the site building aspect of this excellent online service. This is a little more advanced than ZyWeb but there is much more flexibility and ease of use to be had using the SiteMaker control panel.

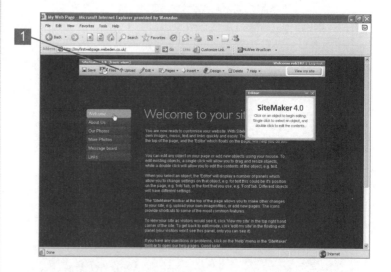

1 The control panel along the top of the window allows you to make structural changes to the site – saving and deleting pages, changing the design, inserting pictures, etc. – whilst you can edit any individual element on a page simply by clicking on the one you want to change.

2 Double click on the main text box to insert your own text. This floating Editor palette allows you to format any of the individual text elements – typefaces, font size, colours and text areas.

3 Double click on the buttons in the navigator bar to bring up tools that allow you to add photos, videos and links.

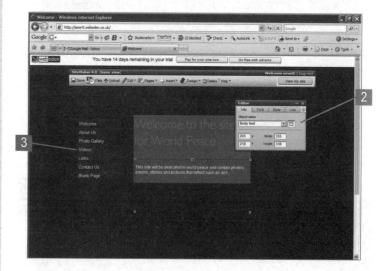

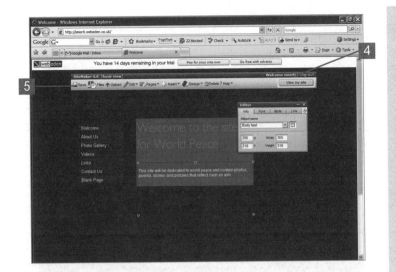

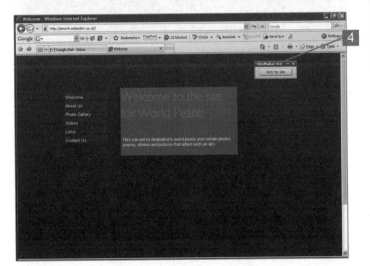

4 Preview your work at any time using the View My Site button in the control panel. If you're not happy with anything, simply jump back into the Editor mode and make any amendments as they are necessary.

5 You will be prompted to save changes regularly but ensure you hit Save before you progress to editing a new page.

3

Important

The floating Editor panel is used to alter the individual elements within a page but you should use the main control panel along the top of the window to carry out more important structural changes to your project, such as saving, adding and removing pages.

Getting your web pages online

As you're using an online service, uploading your pages to the web couldn't be easier.

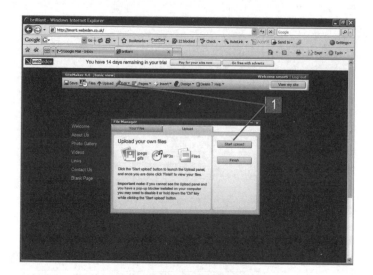

1 If you're happy with the pages you have created, click Upload in the control panel. This opens a File Manager dialog box. Click Start upload.

2 You will be presented with an opportunity to upload additional files from your PC (photos, etc.). All the files will then appear on the web at the address you selected earlier. You should check that everything looks and behaves as expected.

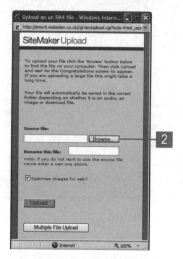

Timesaver tip

When using an online service like this it's a good idea to assemble all of the content (pictures, graphics, PDFs, text files, etc.) that you're going to need *before* you start building and keep it all in one dedicated folder. That way you can be sure all the relevant files are uploaded.

An area of online activity that has become very popular in recent years is the blog. A blog is like a personal diary or journal, usually written by an individual documenting the events in their daily lives, although there are countless variations on that theme. There are lots of options when it comes to creating a blog, but one of the quickest and easiest routes is to use an online service like Blogger.

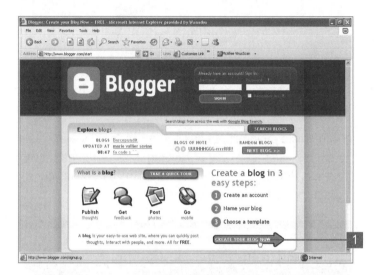

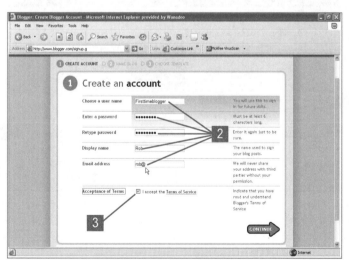

Making your own web blog

1 Go to the Blogger home page at www.blogger.com where you can create a blog of your own in three easy steps. Simply click on the link at the bottom of the page as shown here and you'll be ready to go.

2 You will need to create an account so enter the required information. Don't forget a valid email address and click on Continue when you're done.

3 In order to create an account and start building your very own blog you have to check the Acceptance of Terms checkbox at the bottom of the page. Click on the link if you wish to read the terms first.

3

Making your own web blog (cont.)

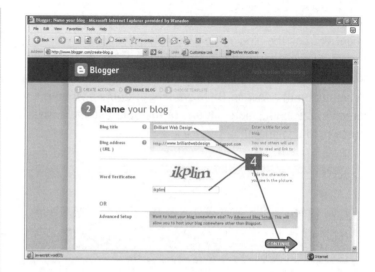

4 You now need to think of a title for your blog so make it something relevant to the subject matter. You will find the web address easier to remember if you pick one that's relevant to the subject too. Type in the Word Verification (a security step) and click Continue.

5 Now you need to select a template for your blog. There is a whole array of these to choose from and you can preview them all first before making a selection. Click on Continue at the bottom of the page when you're ready.

You can create a blog about any subject that you are interested in or simply use it as a way of keeping track of the daily events in your life. Just like your website, you can customise your blog to reflect the subject matter and content.

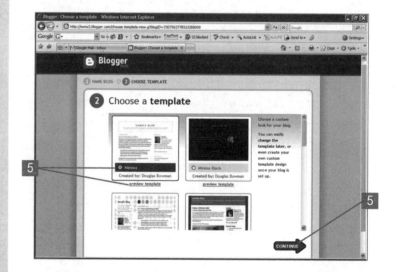

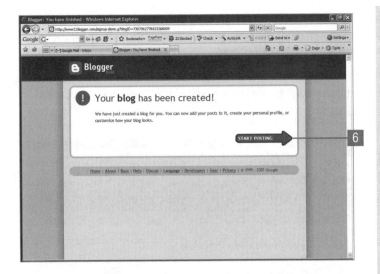

6 Your blog has been created. Start Posting!

7 On the Posting tab, select Create. The editing interface is similar to those we have looked at earlier in the chapter although the tools here are even simpler.

8 You can format your text using the options on the toolbar just above the input window.

9 When you're ready, simply click on Publish Post. You can then view the finished item by clicking on View Blog at the top of the page.

10 Alternatively, save your first draft and use the Settings and Template tabs to make any amendments to the layout of the page that you require.

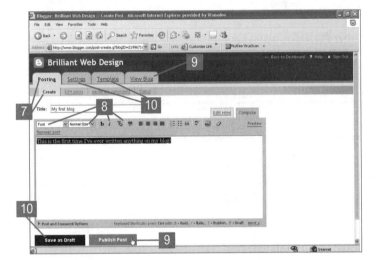

For your information

If you want to make changes to the overall setup up of your blog, such as changing the template that you selected, click on the Back to Dashboard link in the top right-hand corner of the page.

Updating your blog

The secret to a successful blog is to keep it alive. Be sure to make regular updates to the content and remove old or outdated submissions which are no longer needed. Once visitors realise that there are new posts being submitted all the time, they will be much more likely to come back and visit regularly.

1 Once your blog has been generated and you have typed in and submitted some text for the first time you'll see this window appear. It will appear each time you post new content.

2 If you click on View Blog you will be directed to the page you have just created. You'll see that the page design is based on the template you selected and that the date and time of posting is recorded.

3 Once you've created the basic framework of your blog all that you need to do in order to update it is log back in at regular intervals and make new posts. An archive on the right-hand side of the screen records all your postings.

4 Readers of your blog can click on Comments to add their own feedback. The counter here records how many comments have been made.

5 Clicking on the icon by View my Complete Profile will take you to a form where you can easily add any details about yourself you wish to make known, and photos and music too.

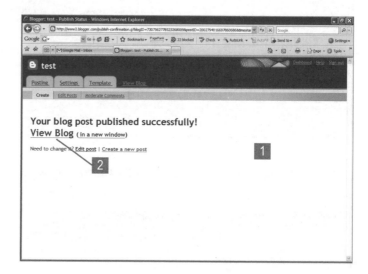

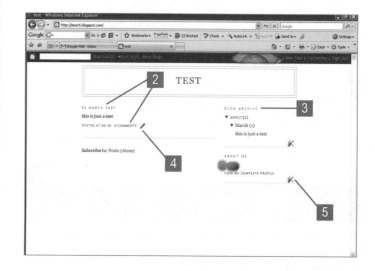

MySpace is a social networking website that allows you to create a personal web page describing you, your hobbies and interests. It hosts it for you, and then links you into a vast network enabling you to interact with friends and internet acquaintances via blogs, bulletin boards, instant messaging and chat rooms. And it's all free!

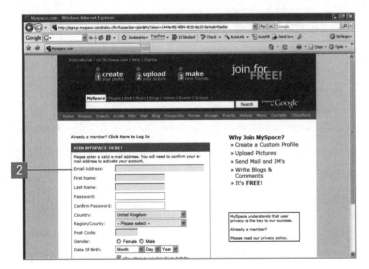

1 To sign up simply go to www.myspace.com and click Sign Up!

2 Fill in the necessary details (note that your password needs to contain at least one numeric character) and click Sign Up again.

3

Creating a MySpace personal home page (cont.)

3 MySpace takes you through a sequence of steps to create your personal web page. You can skip any of the steps and return to them later. The first allows you to upload a photo.

4 Next, invite your friends to join your Space. This is the key to the website's popularity of course. Once you have your own Space, you can search for friends who are already members of the MySpace community.

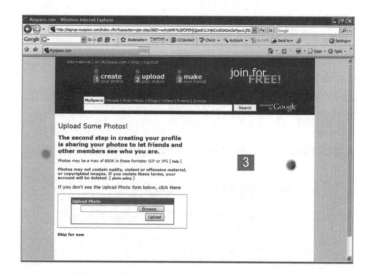

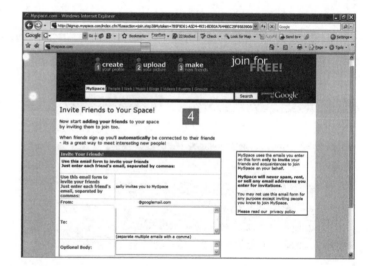

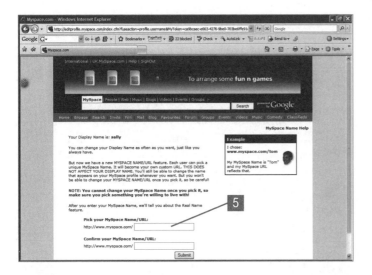

5 Chose your unique URL that you can give to your friends so they can easily find your web page. Note that it has to be unique, but you need to be able to live with it. MySpace won't allow you to change your URL – ever!

6 Welcome to your home page! You will need to verify your email address with a code MySpace sends you by email.

3

Creating a MySpace personal home page (cont.)

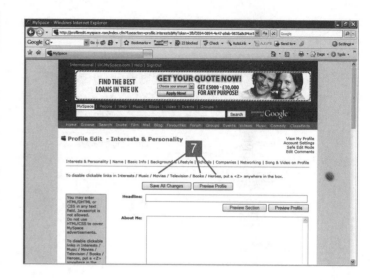

7 Editing your profile is straightforward. Enter all the details you wish on the form under section headings: About me; I'd like to meet; music; films; TV; books; heroes.

For your information

The home pages thus created are necessarily all of a kind – the point is that you're joining a community, not displaying your web design skills. However, the profile pages can be customised using standard HTML tags and you can add videos and Flash-based content in this way. You can also alter the way they look using cascading style sheets – although the way the profiles page is set up means that the browser loads the MySpace default style first and then abruptly changes to your custom layout. There are also several independent online companies that offer MySpace layout design services – similar to those described earlier in this chapter.

Creating a website using FrontPage

Introduction

We've already seen that online web creation services can help you build a perfectly acceptable website, but you may want to build something more unique and tailored to your content. Here we introduce Microsoft's FrontPage. This is widely available either as part of the Office suite or as a standalone product. It even comes pre-installed on some computer systems. The great thing about FrontPage is that it shares many common characteristics with other Microsoft programs. Indeed, you'll find that it boasts similar tools to the likes of Word, Excel and PowerPoint. So if you are familiar with Windows PCs and Microsoft software, then you should find FrontPage very useful. Bear in mind though that there are plenty of other software options – we will discuss these briefly – and that they all employ similar tools to get the job done.

See also

Microsoft has recently released a brand new website creation software package called Expression Web – this is discussed in Chapter 6.

What you'll do

Import web page files

Start a new project

Format your text

Edit colours and layout

Add pictures

Create hyperlinks

Preview your pages

Create additional pages

Add buttons and graphics

Create rollover ALT tags

Investigate alternative software

Importing web page files

If you have been reading this book sequentially, you will already have some web page files created from scratch using HTML, or created in Word or another software package. You don't need to remake these. You can import them into FrontPage and edit them as necessary. Launch FrontPage and you will see that the interface is similar to other Microsoft programs you may be familiar with. What's more, it has many of the same tools in its arsenal.

1 Take a moment to note that the menu options and main toolbars are similar to those you are already familiar with. Even if you opt to use an alternative to Microsoft, you'll find that many of the functions are universal.

2 Down the left-hand side of the main window lie the key features of the program that you will use frequently during the web page construction process.

3 Select File, Open to import any web pages you have already created.

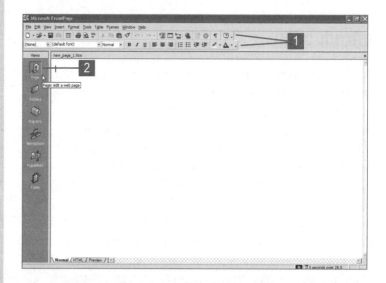

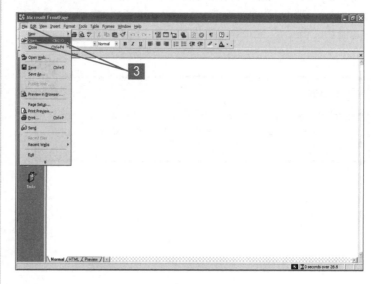

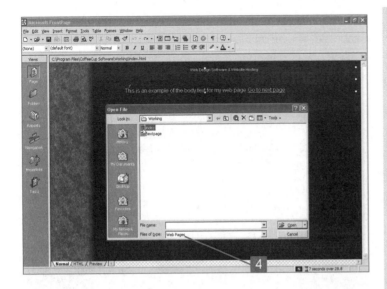

4 Notice that FrontPage searches for Web Pages as the default file type but it is possible to open other documents, such as Word or Rich Text files.

For your information

You can also import other people's web pages. Select File, Open Web…

Starting a new project

FrontPage, in common with the online services we have discussed, allows you to create templates that ensure consistency in design and style throughout your website and save time and effort in the construction process.

1. Select New, Page from the File menu and click on the General tab in the New dialog box.

2. Explore the template options using the thumbnail Preview in the dialog box. Select your preferred design and click OK.

3. The template appears in the main work space. Note the editing mode – the text and pictures are place holders for your own text and pictures and the dotted lines will of course disappear when you Preview the page.

4. The first thing to do is save your new page. Remember to store it in a root directory dedicated to this particular web project. Be sure to give it a unique name to avoid overwriting any other pages.

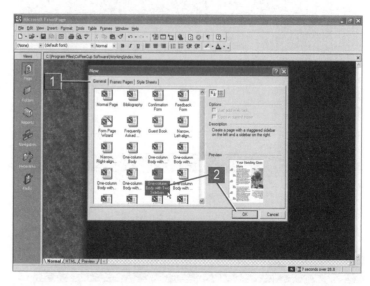

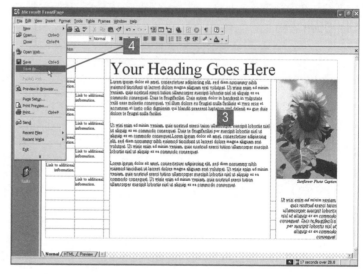

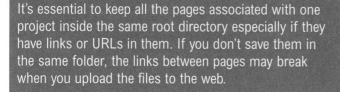

5 Once the page has been saved
you will be able to navigate to
it very easily by clicking on the
Folders icon in the Views
toolbar on the left-hand side
of the screen.

Important

It's essential to keep all the pages associated with one
project inside the same root directory especially if they
have links or URLs in them. If you don't save them in
the same folder, the links between pages may break
when you upload the files to the web.

See also

The other two tabs inside this dialog box allow you to select
frames-based designs and also incorporate style sheets if you
need to. Both of these aspects of web design are dealt with on
pages 150–153 and 157–161 in Chapter 7.

4

Formatting your text

You will be familiar with the text formatting tools as they are identical to those in Word.

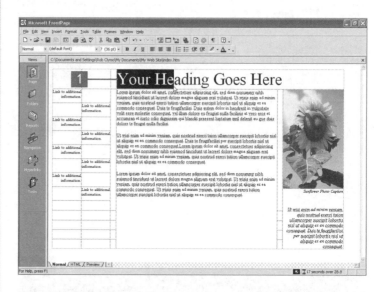

1. Select the text you wish to edit and replace the filler text with your own, either by typing it in or copying and pasting from another document.

2. Format your text as required using the familiar Font, Type size and Styles tools.

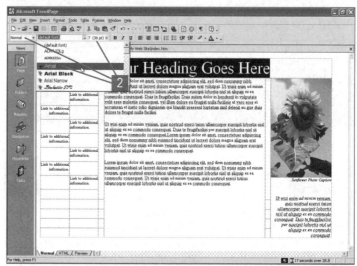

Timesaver tip

Notice that in the bottom left-hand corner of the workspace are three small tabs. These allow you to view your pages in alternative modes: Normal, i.e. editing mode; HTML, i.e. displaying tags; Preview, i.e. the way it will look when viewed through the default browser.

Did you know?

Different web browsers can display fonts in different ways and also in different sizes. Do check the way your pages look in different browsers before uploading them to the web (see pages 137–138 in Chapter 6).

A web page can be a great place for exploring your artistic tendencies! Enjoy exploring the possibilities but take a look at our usability design tips in Chapter 7 before you go live.

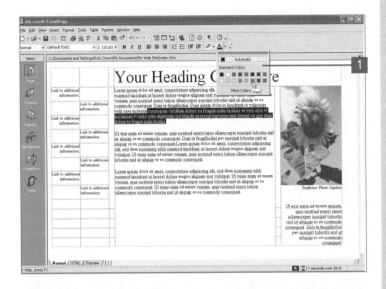

1 A small colour palette allows you to pick a web-friendly shade for your wording.

2 Text alignment is particularly important on a web page where numerous different elements compete for the reader's attention.

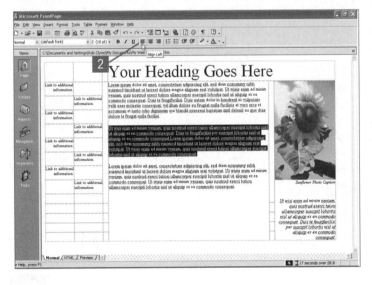

For your information

Save yourself the embarrassment of a typo on your home page and use the spell checker in the Tools menu.

4

Jargon buster

Web safe palette – a subset of commonly used colours that browsers display in a standard way. Colours not contained in this palette may not be viewed in the same way on different browsers.

Adding pictures

Working with the text elements in a web page is one thing, but graphics and other images really bring a web page to life. Adding images to a web page is surprisingly easy. Here's how.

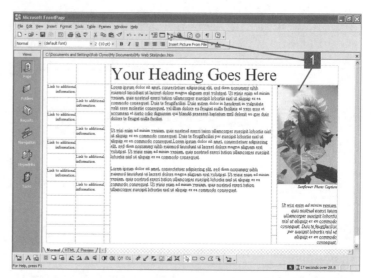

1. The template determines the location of the picture on the page. Select the picture box and click on Insert Picture From File in the toolbar.

2. Select the file you wish to insert (spot the intentional mistake – we should be storing all the files destined for our website in the same root folder, not in random folders distributed throughout the c drive!). Click OK.

3. Note that right clicking on the picture brings up a picture editing toolbar at the bottom of the screen. Use this to rotate, crop, shape and size your picture as necessary.

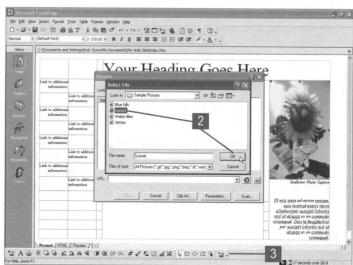

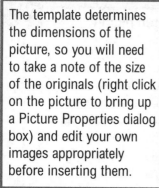

For your information

The template determines the dimensions of the picture, so you will need to take a note of the size of the originals (right click on the picture to bring up a Picture Properties dialog box) and edit your own images appropriately before inserting them.

See also

Creating web-friendly image files from photos and art packages is dealt with on pages 108–118 of Chapter 5.

Pages 88–90 in Chapter 5 explain picture file formats and which to choose for use in web pages.

Links to other pages via URLs allow visitors to explore other areas of your site, or connect to other websites. So, if you've planned properly, you should already have an idea of the links you'll need in your web pages.

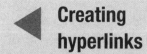
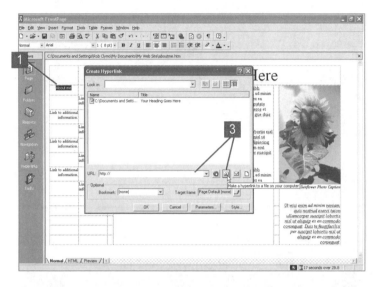

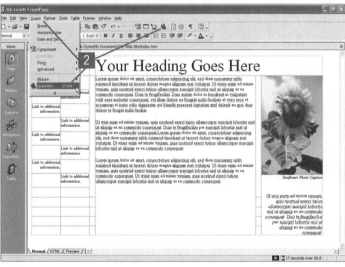

1 Decide on the starting point for the link. Hyperlinks can operate from a section of text, an image or a graphic such as a button. We will create a hyperlink to a personal information page by typing 'About me' into one of the menu slots on the left-hand side of our template.

2 Either click on the small chain icon found in the main toolbar or select Insert, Hyperlink…

3 Select the file (or type in the URL) you wish to connect to. Click OK, and OK again in the Create Hyperlink dialog box.

4

Timesaver tip

Once you've inserted your hyperlink, do a quick test to check it is working as it should. From within FrontPage, simply press Ctrl and click on the link simultaneously and it will be activated.

Creating hyperlinks (cont.)

4 Once you have created the link, the text will be underlined (or, if you created the link from a graphic or button, it will have a coloured boundary around it).

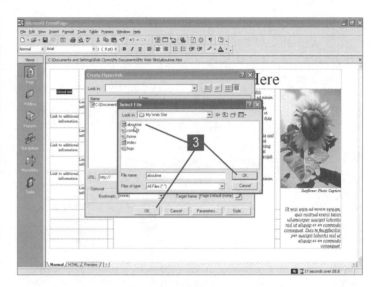

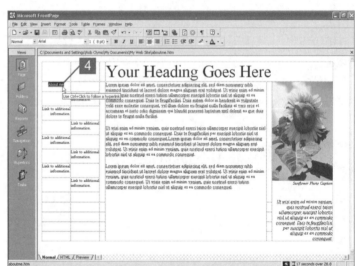

Those three tabs at the foot of the main window give a useful overview of the results each time you make a change to your web page.

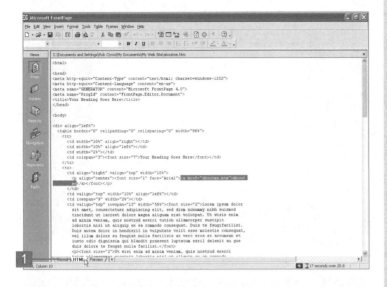

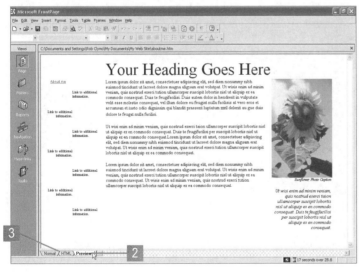

Previewing your pages

1. Although programs like FrontPage remove the need for you to do any of your own HTML coding, use the HTML tab to inspect and understand what happens when you make changes to the content and formatting.

2. Click on the Preview tab in order to see how the finished page will look. Use it to get all of your content and formatting exactly right before you upload it to the internet.

3. Jump back into the page building area by clicking the Normal tab.

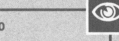

See also

Whilst this is a quick and easy way of checking that your web pages work as intended, remember that this is not an exhaustive test because of the differences in the ways other web browsers read and display page content. We will address how to check final pages more thoroughly on pages 137–138 in Chapter 6.

Timesaver tip

Have a pencil and paper to hand while you're previewing to jot down a 'snagging list' of fixes required when you get back to page building.

Creating additional pages

Working with templates makes it easy to create additional pages that will be identical in format and style to your first.

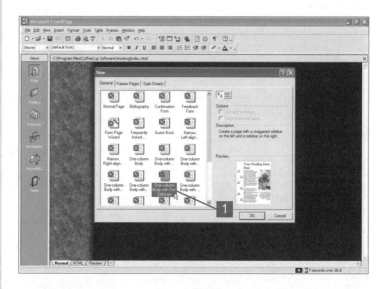

1. If you've not made major changes to the layout and formatting of your initial template page, simply open a new page and select the same template again.

2. If you have made changes that you want to reflect in your new page, having first remembered to save your home page as the 'index', save it again using a name that reflects the content of the new page. We'll create a page containing contact details next and call it 'contactme'.

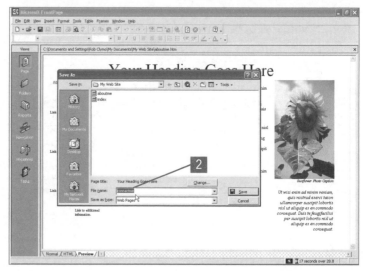

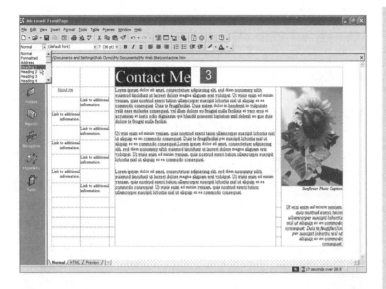

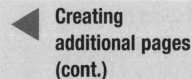
 Generate the content for your new page and format as required.

For your information

Avoid over-the-top formatting schemes. It's a good idea to pick a typeface and basic colour scheme and stick with that throughout your web pages. Make a list of the names and sizes of the fonts you have used to ensure consistency and also jot down the names or numbers of the different colours you have used to ensure the pages all sport the same basic design scheme.

Important

Remember to save each file in the same root directory. FrontPage will automatically generate the .html filename extension.

4

Adding buttons and graphics

Adding buttons, navigation bars and other graphics can make a web page much more appealing. There are plenty of pre-created graphics to choose from that you'll find in your Clip Art collections.

1 Place your cursor in the location you want the graphic to appear and click to select.

2 Select Insert, Picture, Clip Art from the menu. This brings up the Clip Art Gallery which allows you to search the collections and import clips from other files or online sources.

3 The buttons and icons database is handy for abstract graphics.

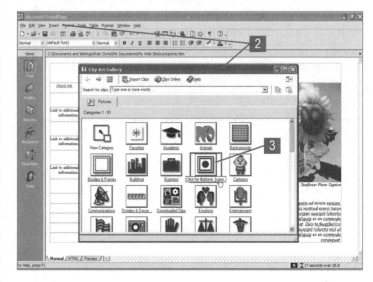

Many of the graphics you use will have a function –
navigational arrows to click forwards and backwards through
the site, buttons to accept or decline an opportunity (e.g. Buy
Now), and icons to represent the content of a particular page.
The function may or may not be clear from the graphic, so it is
sensible to include ALT tags that display the meaning of the
graphic when a mouse hovers over it.

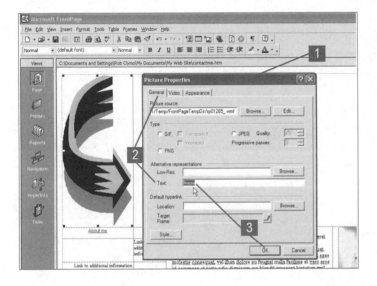

Creating rollover ALT tags

1 Having inserted your graphic
in its correct location, right
click on it to bring up the
Picture Properties dialog box.

2 Select the General tab and
look for the Text option under
Alternative Representations.

3 Type the text that describes
the function of your graphic.
E.g. Type 'next' for arrows that
take the reader forwards, or
'back' for arrows that return to
earlier pages. Click OK.

4

Important

Remember that there is nothing more frustrating for a
reader looking for specific information than a page full
of inexplicable graphics.

Investigating alternative software

CoffeeCup

Budget conscious first-timers should make a beeline for CoffeeCup, located at www.coffeecup.com where you can pick up a copy of their HTML Editor software. This gives you a quick and easy way to write your own HTML code without having to remember all the tags mentioned in Chapter 1. Simply select the tag you need from a list and apply it to your text. The HTML appears in the editor window. You can download a trial and explore what it has to offer before you part with any cash. And when you do come to buy the full version, it can be had for under $50.

NetObjects Fusion

Available at www.netobjects.com, this software is also well worth a look as it has many advanced features – but you need minimal technical knowledge to get the best from its exciting interface. At only £65 it packs a lot of power for its punch.

Did you know?

There are several useful websites that specialise in showing you the range of software applications available for any of the jobs you want to get done. They include reviews and customer feedback on everything from freeware to the expensive professional software applications. If you're up for some browsing, try www.download.com and www.tucows.com.

For your information

Scroll down this page to see a wealth of other software available in free trial versions.

Dreamweaver

Further up the scale is Dreamweaver, which is branded as a professional web design tool but attracts many lower-end users thanks to its friendly interface and sophisticated tool kit. Check it out at www.adobe.com/uk/products/dreamweaver/. Needless to say that for a product so advanced you will need to pay out £400 to own it. The good news though is that 30-day trial versions are available so that you can explore what's on offer and decide if Dreamweaver has what it takes to get the job done. The other benefit is that Macromedia have lots of other products that work in tandem with Dreamweaver, allowing you to build even bigger and better websites.

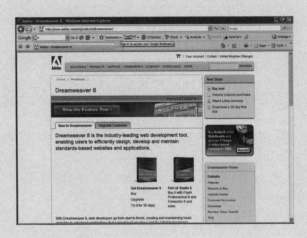

4

Exploring web graphics

Introduction

Now that we've spent some time getting to grips with the basics of web page construction we can turn our sights to something a little more artistic. If you spend any time surfing the internet then you'll know just how much you can spice up a website by adding appropriate graphics. You don't need to have any advanced technical or creative skills to be able to make a real difference to your website. All you need is some software. Appropriate applications range from the basic right through to the technically elaborate. Here we will focus on the basic end of the spectrum so you can be sure that producing colourful content for your web pages can be done both easily and cheaply. You can use Microsoft's Paint program which will probably be pre-installed with your operating system. However, a much more serviceable product is Paint Shop Pro™ from Corel which is a wonderful combination of easy-to-use but powerful tools with an affordable price tag. We'll also point you in the direction of alternative applications as we move through the chapter.

What you'll do

Understand file types

Create a simple banner

Make some buttons

Create lots of similar buttons

Preview your graphics

Incorporate digital photos

Fix your photos

Experiment with graphical effects

Optimise your images for the web

For your information

There are trial versions of most image-editing software programs available online and Paint Shop Pro is no exception. Visit www.corel.com and select the UK site. Here you will be able to click on Try and download a time limited version to explore the many and varied features of the software. If it's what you need, you can purchase it via the secure website. Alternatively, you'll find the boxed product in most computer retail outlets.

Understanding file types

The secret to success with graphics lies in understanding the various file formats along with their relative strengths and weaknesses. There are 3 main file formats that are used on the web: GIF, JPEG and PNG. These are industry standard formats and should be used in preference to any other file types your software may offer.

GIFs

GIF (Graphics Interchange Format) files use a palette of up to 256 distinct colours to produce an image. This makes them ideal for images such as logos, navigation bars and buttons which use solid blocks of colour. They are not suitable for colour photographs or images that use continuous colour. GIF files are compressed using a lossless compression technique that generates a smaller file without losing visual quality. They are therefore quick and easy to download – a factor of vital importance in creating websites that don't leave your readers waiting. You can generate solid colour GIF files easily using the basic colour palette in a software program like Paint. And you can create custom colours too.

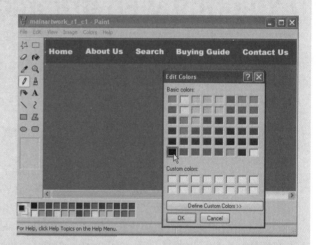

Timesaver tip

Create an 'images' sub-folder in your root directory in which to store all your graphics.

JPEGs

The JPEG format was tailor made for photographic images – it specifies both the way in which the colours are transformed into bytes, and the format used to contain them. It uses a lossy compression technique which means that although some visual quality is lost, the resulting file has sufficient resolution to make it look good on screen and it is quick to download, making it ideal for use on websites. The lossy compression, however, makes such files unsuitable for line drawings, icons and textual graphics. The sample pictures that are pre-installed in your 'My Pictures' directory are JPEGs. Right click on the picture and select Properties to confirm. They may be edited using the standard tools in Paint to produce handy little graphics to liven your website.

Timesaver tip

One of the biggest errors you can commit in website design is forcing the reader to download too many data-rich images. Image editing software packages, like those described in this chapter, make it very easy to shave off unwanted data from your files without affecting their quality. For the sake of your readers, don't ignore this vital aspect of design.

Did you know?

You can use the magnifying glass tool in the toolbar on the left-hand side of the screen to zoom into a particular area of the image. The individual pixels that make up the picture will become quite clear illustrating that onscreen viewing does not require very high image resolution – a fact to keep in mind when saving digital photos for use on your website.

Understanding
file types (cont.)

PNGs

The PNG (Portable Network Graphics) format was created to improve upon GIF and also employs lossless compression. It was created specifically for transferring files on the internet so it supports the screen-friendly RGB colour palette and is not suitable for professional printing. It is ideal for line drawings, icons and other solid colour graphics as it preserves sharp edges and it is not limited to the 256 colours of GIF files.

Jargon buster

PNG – short for Portable Network Graphics – this format was created to improve upon GIF. It was created specifically for transferring files on the internet so it supports the screen-friendly RGB colour palette and is not suitable for professional printing. It is ideal for line drawings, icons and other solid colour graphics as it preserves sharp edges and it is not limited to the 256 colours of GIF files.

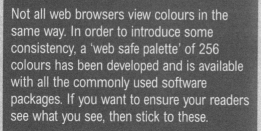

Important

Not all web browsers view colours in the same way. In order to introduce some consistency, a 'web safe palette' of 256 colours has been developed and is available with all the commonly used software packages. If you want to ensure your readers see what you see, then stick to these.

Although you can find lots of pre-created graphics in Clip Art collections, it's so easy to create your own that we encourage you to give it a go. We'll use Paint Shop Pro to demonstrate how straightforward creating a simple banner can be.

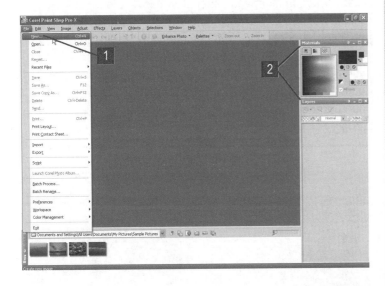

Creating a simple banner using Paint Shop Pro

1 Open Paint Shop Pro. Select File, New…

2 Notice the tool palettes on the right-hand side of the window. The Layers and Materials palettes will come in handy for this project. If they are not currently being displayed, you can bring them up by selecting View, Palettes and choosing those you want displayed. You can drag them around your workspace as required.

Did you know?

Constructing complex images is made easy in Paint Shop Pro by using layers. Think about a picture starting with a canvas, or background layer that contains colour, texture or pattern. The picture is then built up in layers that contain the main image (a person perhaps), some text (a caption for example) and further digital adjustments. The layers palette helps you to manage these layers by giving them names, allowing you work on them individually, duplicate and delete them and to change their positions in the stack. The layers are 'flattened out', or merged, to create a final image for saving as a JPEG or for printing.

For your information

You can specify sizes in centimetres, inches or pixels. The pixel is the most commonly used standard in website construction.

5

Creating a simple banner using Paint Shop Pro (cont.)

3 To make it really easy, the Presets drop-down menu contains a whole range of standard sized features such as buttons, navigation bars and banners. We will select the 234 × 60 Half Banner. Note that the size is specified in pixels. Also note that the resolution is specified in pixels/inch. For use on screen, resolution does not normally need to exceed 100 pixels/inch (72 or 96 'dots per inch' are the most commonly used). For printing, the resolution needs to be higher.

4 Next you need to select your background layer. Choose the Raster Background and use the drop-down menu by Colour depth to select RGB (8 bit) or 256 Colours – remembering that the key here is to create a quickly downloadable graphic that you can save as a GIF file.

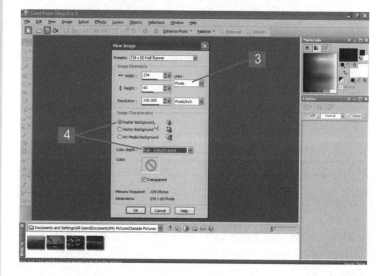

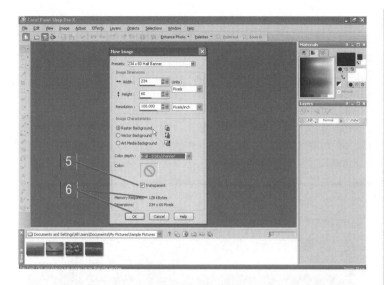

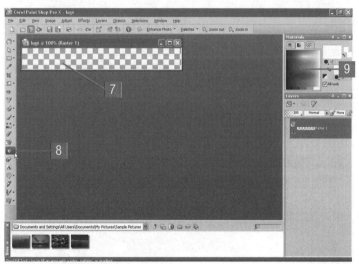

5. We will select the Transparent option rather than a coloured background but uncheck the Transparent box if you wish and click on the Colour box to be presented with a palette of colours to chose from.

6. Take a note of the Memory Required for your choice to ensure you are not creating a huge image file that will take a long time to download. Click OK.

7. Your file will appear in the main workspace. The chequered effect shows that the background is transparent. Save this before you start adding anything to it. Save it as a PSP image file for the moment – this means that it is editable. We'll look at exporting the right file type for use on the web later on.

8. Just for fun, we will now use the Flood Fill Tool located in the left-hand toolbar to make the background white.

9. Select the tool and then click on the shade you require in the Materials palette.

Did you know?

A file saved in the Paint Shop Pro (PSP) image file format might not be recognised by another graphics program, but Bitmap files (extension .bmp) are recognised by most software.

Exploring web graphics 93

Creating a simple banner using Paint Shop Pro (cont.)

10 To apply the colour to the background of your image simply keep the Flood Fill Tool selected and then click inside the graphic.

Adding text

1 Click on the Text Tool (the letter 'A' in the left hand toolbar).

2 Type the text you require into the Text Entry box.

3 Select View, Palettes, Tool Options and a toolbar that gives you options related to the tool you have in use will appear.

Timesaver tip

If you need to match the colour of your graphic exactly, this is best done at the beginning using the New Image dialog box. You can manually select the exact colour by clicking in the Colour box – but note that you may need to de-restrict your colour range from 256 to 16 Million Colours (24 bit) thus making your file potentially larger.

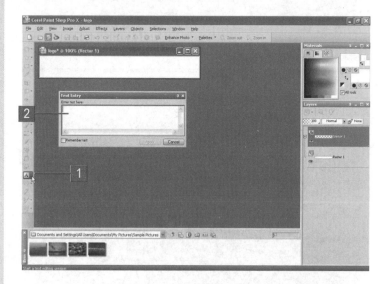

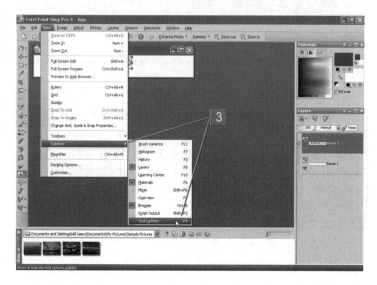

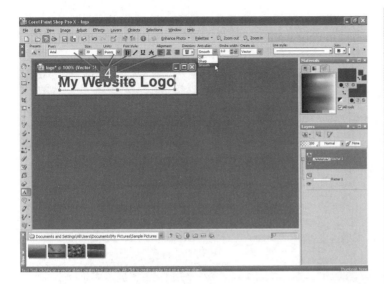

Creating a simple banner using Paint Shop Pro (cont.)

4 Use these options to select font, size, style, alignment, orientation (horizontal or vertical) and line width. Click Apply. Notice that this automatically creates a new Vector layer for the text on your image. The size and shape of the textbox can be changed without affecting the background layer.

5 Save your banner using an appropriate name in the graphics sub-folder of your root directory.

Jargon buster

Bitmap – a simple graphics file format used by Microsoft Windows software.

5

Making some navigation buttons

These little graphics will help you to spice up the links between pages in your website.

1. Select File, New. From the Presets drop-down menu in the New Image dialog box, select the 88 x 31 Micro Button.

2. Select 256 (8 bit) Colour Depth and click OK.

3. Use the Flood Fill Tool to create a coloured background. You can create gradients and patterns using the Materials palette too, although these might perhaps be lost on such a small graphic!

4. Use the Text Tool to name the button after the task it will perform. Here for example, it will take people back to the home page when clicked on.

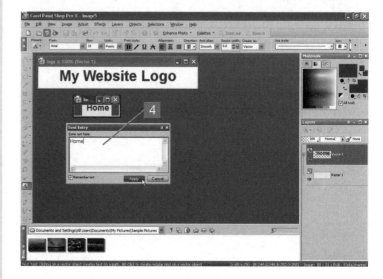

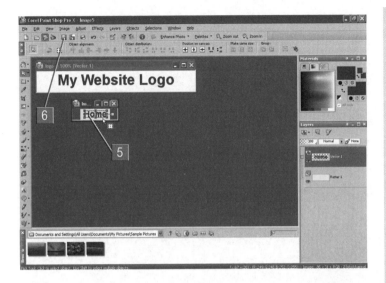

5 Use the handles on the textbox to drag and rotate the text, stretch or resize the textbox as necessary.

6 Save your button giving it an easily recognisable name such as 'HomeButton' in the graphics sub-folder of your root directory.

Timesaver tip

Have a list of the different buttons you'll need for your web page so that you can create them all at the same time. This means that they will then have a neat and consistent look that'll fit in with the rest of your design when it comes to putting everything together.

Creating lots of similar buttons

If you are creating lots of similar graphics all at the same time then the Layers palette can make the process very quick. For example, with buttons, all you need to do is amend the text layer each time you want to change the name of the button, retaining all the work you have done on size, background and shape.

1 Save your button file several times (using File, Save As…) to create exact duplicates of your original, giving them appropriate names such as ContactButton, BackButton, etc.

2 Open each file in turn, select the Vector layer containing the text and click on the original text to bring up the Text Entry window.

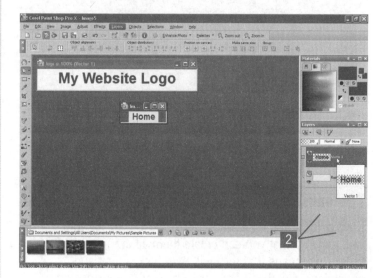

Timesaver tip

Remember that if you are working with lots of images at the same time then you can stow them away without closing them down entirely by clicking on the small Minimize box at the top right-hand corner of the window, just as you would in any other Windows program.

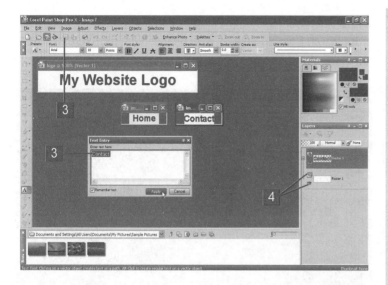

3 The original text will be displayed in the Text Entry window. Delete this and replace it with your new text. Format the text as necessary. Resave the file. Now you have two consistently styled buttons. NB. If, in step 2, you clicked inside the button but not on the original text, the Text Entry window will be clear and anything you type in will appear on the button *in addition* to your original text.

4 There are additional tools in the Layers palette which are worth exploring. Clicking on the eye will temporarily hide a layer so you can see the content of the others more clearly. Clicking on the Opacity icon gives you the opportunity to fade one layer into another.

Important

While you are in the process of creating and editing graphics, it is important to save any iterations of your design process as clearly named files in the Paint Shop Pro (PSP) format. This format maintains the individual layers and ensures the file is editable. Once you save the file into a web-ready format such as JPEG or GIF, the layers will be merged and you will no longer be able to edit them one at a time

5

Exploring web graphics 99

Previewing your graphics

It is useful while you're working to be able to preview your graphics and get an idea of how they will look on screen. There are a couple of alternative options here:

1 For a quick look at how your chosen colours and textures work together and how well the text is positioned, select View, Full Screen Preview (or press Ctrl+Shift+A). This displays the button on a black background. Click or press any key to return to the workspace.

2 In order to see how your graphic will look from inside a browser, select View, Preview In Web Browser... The dialog box allows you to select the browser you want to check it in (you have to have it installed on your machine), the image format you plan to use for the button (GIF is ideal for buttons, bars and icons), and the background colour of the screen. Select Preview.

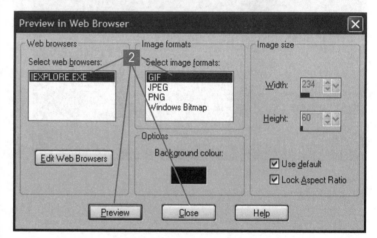

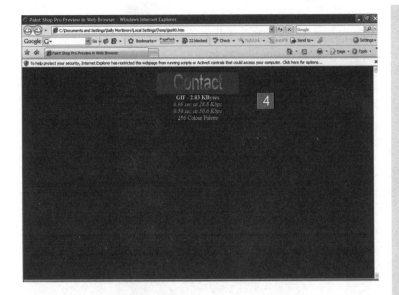

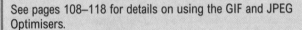

3 The GIF (or JPEG) Optimiser window will be dealt with in more detail later in the chapter. For now, just click on OK.

4 As well as showing you how the button will look, the software tells you how big the final file will be and how long it will take to download.

See also

See pages 108–118 for details on using the GIF and JPEG Optimisers.

5

Incorporating digital photos

The best way to make a website personal is to add a photograph or two. Digital cameras and editing software make it easy to import photographs onto your PC. Alternatively, you can scan from a printed copy.

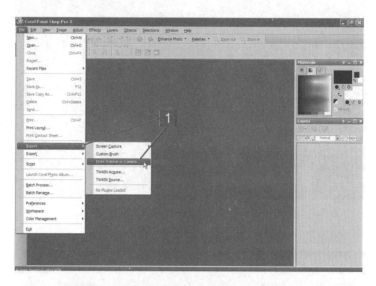

Importing pictures from your camera

1 In the File menu select Import, From Scanner or Camera...

2 Click on the Browser palette option found on the left of the toolbar at the top of the window – this allows you to preview as thumbnails along the bottom of the screen, all of the images you've imported.

3 Click on the image you wish to work on. This is a handy way of managing pictures and deciding which ones you want to use in your website.

4 There is a selection of useful image management tools to be found in the toolbar along the top of the browser palette. Hover your cursor over each of them to see a short description of what they do. Using these will speed up your workflow, especially if you have a lot of images to view.

Some of the images will probably be orientated wrongly (as you've rotated the camera to take a 'portrait' view). This is easily fixed.

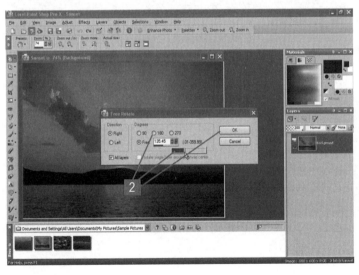

Rotating images

1 Select the Image menu to view a selection of different options for rotating your image. You can turn the picture in 90° steps to the left or right or use the Free Rotate option to do it manually.

2 The Free Rotate option allows you rotate the image very precisely. Use the Degrees settings to specify the rotation required, or alternatively use the slider to make even more gradual changes to the way your image sits on the screen. Click OK.

5

Fixing your photos

Paint Shop Pro is a great tool for both beginners and more experienced users alike because while there are plenty of tool options available that allow you to twiddle and tweak endlessly, there are also several 'one click' options that apply quick fixes in seconds. The One Step Photo Fix option is particularly useful.

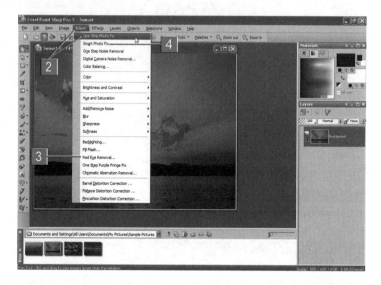

1 Select File, Open and browse to the image file containing the photo you wish to adjust. Double click to open it within the workspace.

2 Save your file under a new name and select Adjust, One Step Photo Fix. Do you like the result?

3 Explore the additional editing tools available – the Red Eye Removal... tool is particularly useful.

4 The Smart Photo Fix... tool is a similarly quick way of making adjustments to your shot but this one gives you a bit more manual control over the final image allowing you to preview changes before they are applied.

Important

Remember that before you make any changes to your digital images it's a good idea save the file under a new name so that, should anything go drastically wrong, you can always return to the untouched original.

5 If you're not sure about, for
example, the level of
Saturation you're after, use the
Suggest Settings button to
give you a clue.

Experimenting with graphical effects

Have some fun using the very simple but effective Effects Browser to transform your photos into arty images you can use as backgrounds, buttons and icons on your website.

1 The Effects menu contains a range of fascinating graphical tricks that can be applied to an image and each one contains a further range of options.

Timesaver tip

Effects can be incrementally added on top of one another and it's easy to lose track of what you've done, so make a note as you go along of the settings you have applied if there is any chance you will want to replicate them on further images.

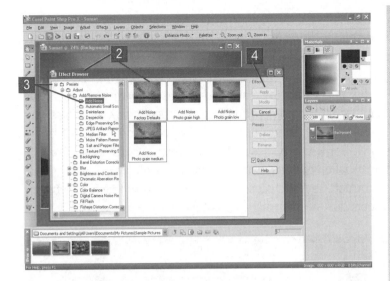

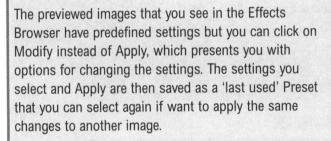

2 If you haven't used this kind of tool before, select the Effects Browser which displays thumbnails of the images resulting from each effect using different preset settings.

3 Select from the range of effects and their various options and presets using the menu on the left-hand side of the window.

4 Select the kind of image you require and click Apply. The new image will appear in the workspace. You can then manipulate the settings further by selecting the appropriate tool in the original menu.

Timesaver tip

The previewed images that you see in the Effects Browser have predefined settings but you can click on Modify instead of Apply, which presents you with options for changing the settings. The settings you select and Apply are then saved as a 'last used' Preset that you can select again if want to apply the same changes to another image.

5

Optimising your images for the web

1. Select View, Toolbars, Web.

2. The Web toolbar contains some useful features that will allow you to make some final adjustments to your graphics files and create web-ready images.

Thanks to another labour-saving toolbar in Paint Shop Pro, getting your images ready for the web is easy. This is a process called web optimisation in which you firstly remove any unwanted data from the image and then compress the rest of your image data to create a small and easily downloadable file. As we touched on previously you'll need to save your files in one of three file formats: JPEG for photographs and GIF or PNG for web graphics with large areas of solid colour like navigation buttons, bars and logos. Saving your graphics files correctly is a vital step in ensuring that your finished website operates as efficiently as possible.

Jargon buster

Wizard – a part of the user interface that leads the user step-by-step through a complex task using a series of dialog boxes.

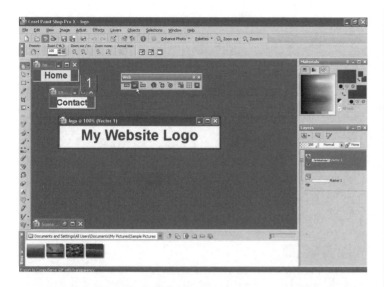

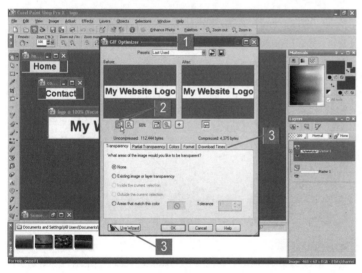

GIF files

1 For icons, buttons and navigation bar graphics, click on the GIF icon to open the GIF Optimiser window.

2 Zoom in and out of the graphic using these small magnifying glass icons if the image doesn't fit in the small preview windows.

3 The options here are numerous but the Wizard will give you a step-by-step guide to deciding on settings for transparency and colours. (Click on Download Times to discover how long your file will take to download.)

5

Optimising your images for the web (cont.)

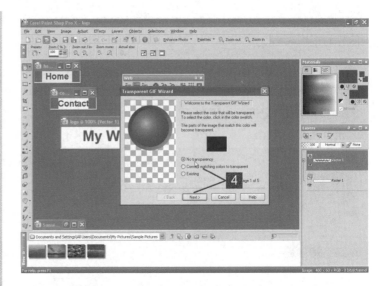

4 Use the radio buttons to select which parts of your image you would like to be transparent. You may wish to convert to transparent any colours in your graphic that exactly match the background of your web page, thereby reducing the data in your image file without affecting the look of the final image. Click Next.

5 Use this slider to reduce the number of colours in your graphic – you can chose to use fewer than 256 if you wish and the resulting file will be smaller. Click Next.

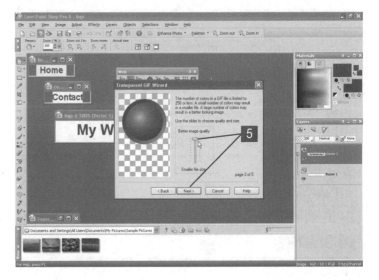

Important

Remember that while reducing the number of colours in an image will dramatically reduce the size of your file, it may also have a detrimental effect on the overall quality of the graphic so it's worth having a trial run before you save the file properly to ensure a good compromise.

Optimising your images for the web (cont.)

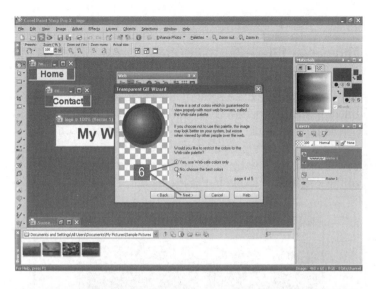

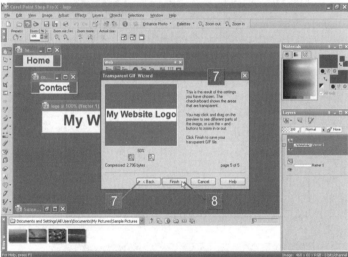

6 Opt to use the web safe palette if you want to ensure your website looks identical across browsers. Click Next.

7 Preview the settings you have chosen. You can return to previous dialog boxes to change your decisions.

8 Click Finish and you will be prompted to save your adjusted and optimised image in GIF format.

5

Optimising your images for the web (cont.)

For your information

The process for saving a PNG file works in much the same way as the GIF. So, once you have completed this set of steps, you can also use the same principles to experiment with the PNG file format and see if it produces a leaner file than the GIF format.

Timesaver tip

Once you've selected ideal settings for the image you want to optimise, these settings are saved as a 'Last Used' Preset. If you envisage working on files over a period of days, you can save the settings as, for example, a 'Button' preset, allowing you to optimise and save them consistently. Click on Options to display a list of the settings included in the Preset.

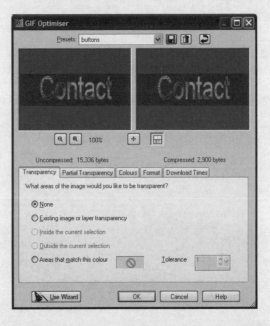

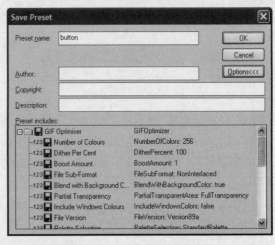

There are some other nifty tools in the Web toolbar that you may wish to use *before* you optimise your GIF file to create really professional looking web graphics.

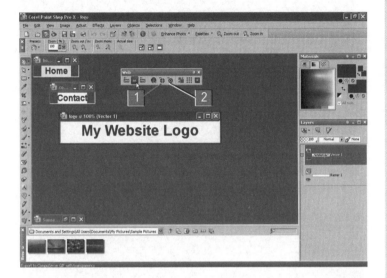

Jargon buster

Image map – a picture with several hyperlinks attached to different areas so that the one picture can be the route to many places.

Making use of the Web toolbar

1 The image slicer enables you to divide an image into several smaller images that you can save in different formats and at different levels of optimisation. The location of each slice of the image is saved so that images are reassembled when the user downloads the web page. This allows you to save a section that appears in lots of different images (a logo for example) only once and thus decrease the size of the files to be downloaded. This tool also allows you to create a Rollover – an image or section of an image that changes appearance when the user activates it or moves a mouse over it. Web designers frequently create rollovers for the buttons of a navigation bar.

2 The image mapper allows you to create a defined region of an image (a circle, rectangle or irregular shape) that links to a URL. When the user moves the mouse over the region, the cursor transforms into a hand indicating that it is a link to another page.

5

Optimising your images for the web (cont.)

3 The seamless tiling tool is quite handy for creating background images for your web pages. You could use this to create a repeated pattern featuring your logo for example.

4 The buttonise tool creates wonderfully three dimensional buttons from your flat images in a single click.

The JPEG Optimiser is used for images that contain continuous colour, such as photographs, allowing you to retain much of the picture detail and quality whilst minimising the amount of data in the file. The trick is to find the ideal combination of file size and picture quality. This will obviously depend on what you aim to use the pictures for. If they are there purely to decorate the site, quality may not be too important, but if they are illustrating something you wish to sell, quality becomes a higher priority.

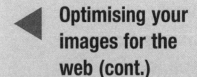

JPEG files

1 For photographs and other continuous colour graphics, open the JPEG Optimiser window.

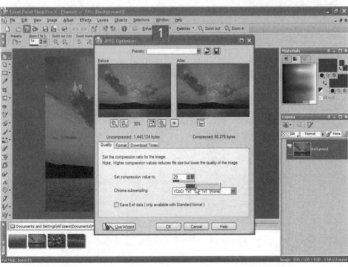

5

Optimising your images for the web (cont.)

[2] The Wizard takes you through steps to select the compression ratio (the higher the value, the smaller the file and the lower the final quality of the photo) and whether you wish to deactivate Chroma Subsampling.

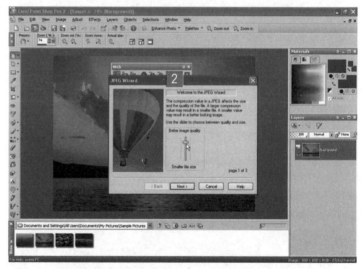

Important

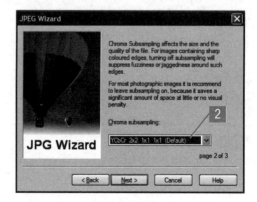

Due to the way JPEG compression works, you will not be able to reverse the effects of compressing your image once it has been saved. Be sure to give your final, optimised image a new name so you don't overwrite your original.

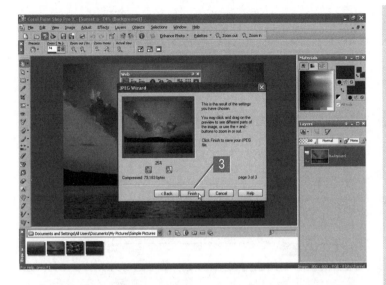

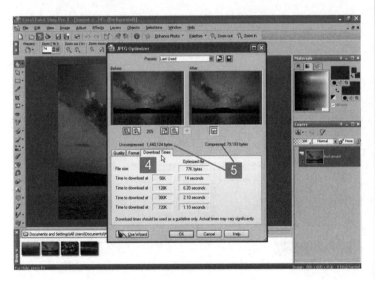

3 Use the preview to experiment with different values. Click Finish and you will be prompted to save your optimised file as a JPEG.

4 Having used the wizard once or twice, you may wish to revert to selecting your settings manually as this allows you to see how your choices affect the Download Times for different connection speeds.

5 Note that the relative sizes (in bytes) of the compressed and uncompressed files are provided each time you make a selection.

5

Optimising your images for the web (cont.)

6 For most photographic images it is best to leave subsampling on because it saves a significant amount of file space with little or no affect on the visual quality. However, for pictures containing sharp, coloured edges, you may wish to turn it off to reduce fuzziness or jaggedness around the edges.

7 The Format tab gives you a further option to help the user if you are selecting higher quality, larger file sizes. You can encode the JPEGs as Progressive instead of the default Standard. This makes a lower quality image appear quite quickly which then progressively upgrades itself – less frustrating for the user than watching a blank space.

8 Remember to save your settings as an aptly named Preset if you wish to replicate them on a series of pictures.

Creating a website using Expression Web Designer

6

Introduction

Expression Web Designer is a part of Microsoft's Expression range, a collection of separately available programs that cover all the bases of developing smart-looking websites. Expression Web provides a complete and efficient environment for coding modern web pages, allowing you to create them with little coding knowledge.

You can either create a page using your existing coding skills or type the text you want to appear – styling it up as you would in a word processor and allowing Expression to create the correct code for you. This chapter provides a guide to creating a simple page in Expression Web, showing off the power and speed of the program's development tools.

As a new product on the market, Expression has all the features of its rivals as well as having developed a smart interface with a simpler way of putting all these features in your hands. Expression is the successor to FrontPage for developers of impressive websites and web professionals. Another product, Office SharePoint Designer is aimed at those creating content and sharing information within a business.

Downloading Expression Web

Expression Web is available as a downloadable purchase or to buy in computer stores. You can also download a free 60-day trial version if you wish to give the program a test before you make a buying decision. In either case, installation follows the standard Windows format with a couple of extras to watch out for. Windows XP users may need to download and install an extra set of system files and there are a couple of choices you can make, before beginning to use the program. If you download Web Expression then you will be emailed a registration key that you will be required to enter.

1 Go to www.microsoft.com/products/expression/ to find out more about Expression Web and to download the demo. Click on the Expression Web box to find out more about this part of the Expression range. Scroll down the page to read more about the program.

2 Click on the Free Trial Download link to download a 60-day free version of Expression Web.

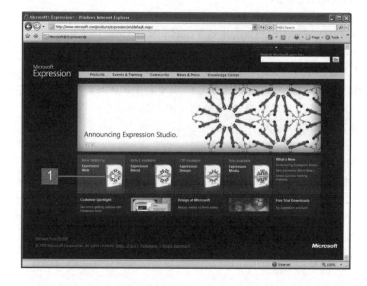

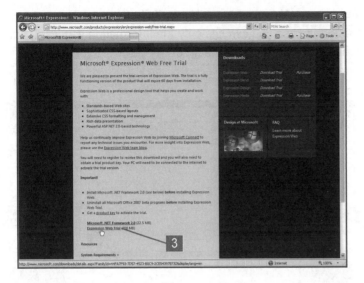

3 The file is 200Mb and will take about 10 minutes over a broadband connection. Once downloaded, the file installs as a normal Windows application.

Important

NetFX 2.0 is an integral part of Microsoft's online coding scheme and is a required install for Expression Web Designer to work. If you downloaded Expression you will need to get this 20MB file, available on the same download page and install it before Expression.

Finding your way around Expression Web

Expression Web is a busy program full of features. It can be customised so you can see only the information you want, but when you start it up for the first time you will see a screen similar to this.

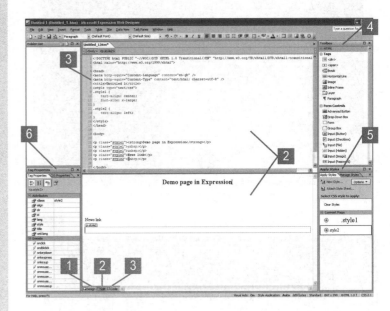

1. The Design View lets you type in text as you would a word processor, the code is automatically created for you.

2. In Split View (shown) you can see both the HTML code and what the page will look like.

3. Code view shows a full page of the coded version of your work in progress.

4. In the Toolbox is a list of all of your commands, from HMTL tags to forms and other web elements.

5. The Styles box stores different variations of font and colour so you can quickly apply different styles to pages.

6. The Tag Properties shows all the different attributes you can apply to an element on the page.

Expression Web is a highly flexible program you can tailor to your working needs. You can move the tools and frames in Expression wherever you like on the screen to adjust the workspace and ensure the tools you use most are to hand. As Expression is based on FrontPage, many of the themes will appear familiar in this chapter.

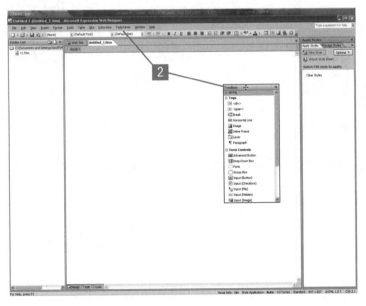

1 The main part of the screen is the Design View which can be set to the size of the web page you want to work in. Change this by going to View, Page Size and choosing the appropriate dimensions.

2 Around the main part of the Page are the Task Panes. To choose which ones you have displayed, click on the Task Panes menu, tick ones you wish to see and untick those you do not. You can move Task Panes around the screen by clicking and dragging. The pane will dock smartly into position wherever you drop it.

Changing the layout of the interface (cont.)

3 You can resize a Task Pane by moving the cursor to the edge of a pane until you see the Resize icon. Now hold down the left mouse button and drag the pane into the size you want. This can make it easier to see longer commands or more of a large list of options.

4 Should you decide you don't like the changes you've made you can undo them and return the workspace to its default state. Go to the Task Panes menu and click the last option on the list, Reset Workspace Layout.

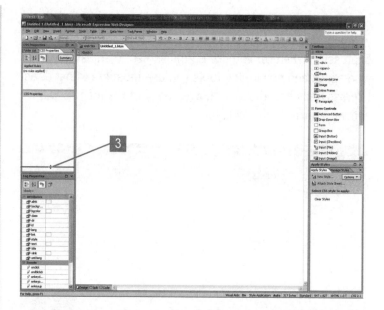

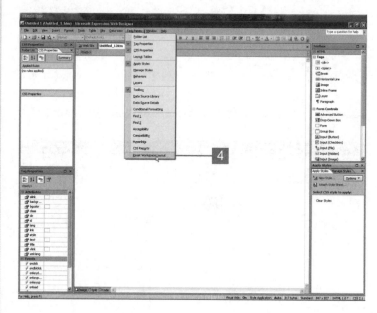

The simplest way to get started with Expression is to use a template. These come in a range of styles and designs and can provide the starting point for your own creations, or you can save time and effort and customise them for use in your own site. Expression includes templates for personal, business and organisational sites – further examples can be downloaded from the Expression website. A thumbnail preview allows you to browse the layout and design features of a site without opening each document in turn. The templates also contain examples of master pages and CSS style sheets which you can use to develop your knowledge of how these schemes work.

1 Click on File, New, Web Site to open the Templates dialog box.

See also

See pages 157–161 for more information on CSS style sheets.

Using a web template (cont.)

2 Click on the Templates entry in the left-hand column.

3 The list of available templates appears in the centre.

4 You can see a preview of the design and other information in the right-hand column.

5 You can choose where to save your new website using the Browse button.

6 When you choose a location, the folder list appears, with all the pages, links and images of the new site.

7 Double click on the master.dwt file to open the master page in Design View.

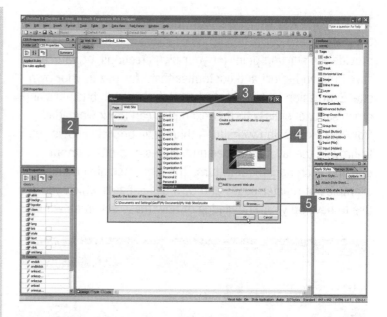

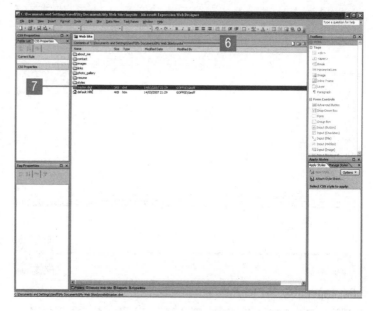

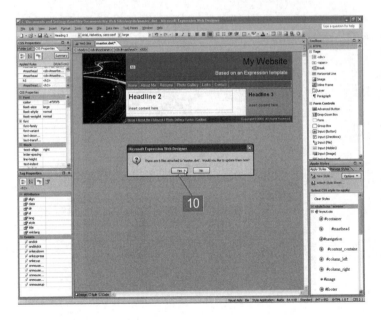

8 Click on an area of the master page template to edit and start entering your own information.

9 Select File, Save.

10 You will see an alert about attached files. Click Yes to update them.

Using a web template (cont.)

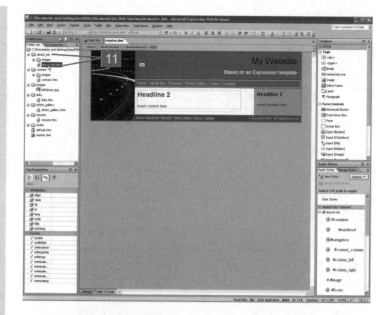

11 Click on the about_me folder in the Folder List and double-click on the about_me.htm file.

12 You will see that the information you changed in the master file has updated on this page too, highlighting the power of the master page.

13 You can edit the body text of the page and choose new images for the page.

14 Areas of the page you cannot edit, those that belong to the master file for example, will show a warning circle icon when you hold the cursor over them.

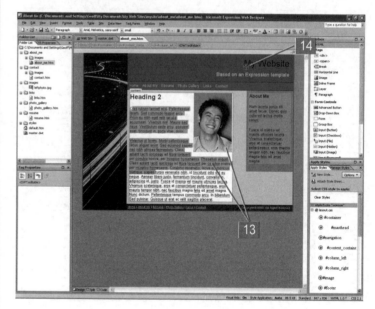

You may have tried out many other web development tools and applications in your quest to create a website and you'll be relieved to know this work is not wasted. You can import your files into Expression and export Expression files into other packages. There are several ways to achieve this task, the simplest being the use of the Web Package file format. This is supported by most web development tools and takes all the required files from a site and stores them in a single archive, making transferring between applications straightforward. Other solutions include importing a site file by file, either from a hard disk or by recovering the file from your FTP site.

1 Select Import from the File menu. If you just need to import files from your own PC, select File...

2 If you want to import files from a site that's online, choose Import Site Wizard.

Importing an existing web page file (cont.)

3. Choose the way you wish to retrieve your file, the most likely method is via FTP.

4. For FTP, enter the site name and directory in the spaces provided.

5. Enter your user name and password so the program can recover the files from the FTP site.

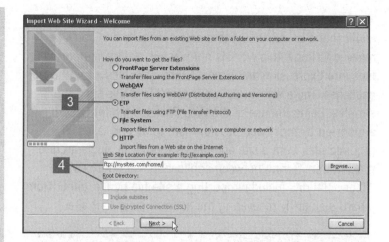

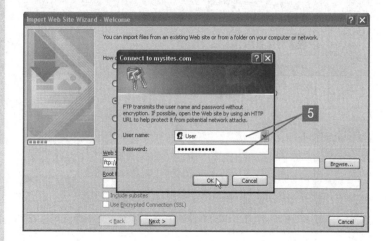

The simplest way to construct a web page in Expression is to type directly into the Design Space. The text formatting features will be familiar to you if you use any other Windows software. All the formatting will be encoded by the program so that when you switch to look at the Code Space, you will see the HTML commands that make your text appear in the same style in any browser.

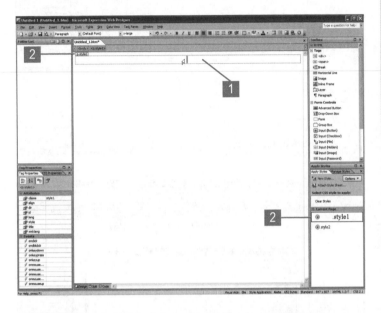

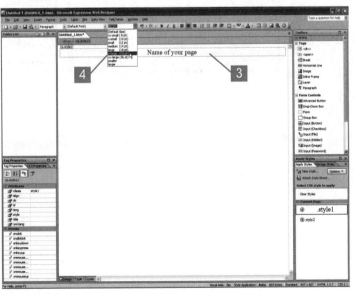

1 Click at the top of the Design Space window and a wide border will appear.

2 You can see at the top left that it is known as 'p.style1', this is its CSS style reference. This reference is stored so you can easily apply the same style you give this part of the page to any other text features.

3 Type in the name of your page. As the text is editable you can come back and change it at any point.

4 Change the text style to make it stand out. You can use different fonts, sizes and text effects.

Starting a new project (cont.)

5 Click further down the page and additional lines appear where you can enter more text.

6 If you want to style an element quickly, use the list of pre-formatted styles

7 Save your page in the root directory where you are storing all the files for your website.

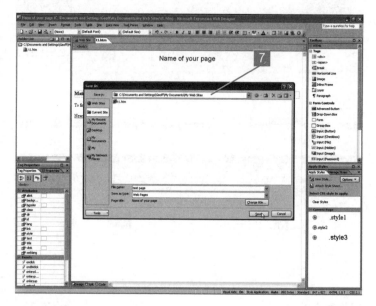

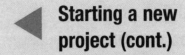
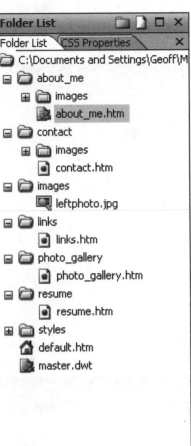

8 Pick a suitable file name for each page you create. For sites with many pages a formal structure will help you arrange and access them easily.

Adding pictures and creating hyperlinks

Incorporating additional features such as pictures, graphics and hyperlinks is very straightforward.

1. Use the Picture function on the Insert menu to add a picture or graphic. Browse your folders to find the picture and it will be added to the page. Move and resize the image to fit the page.

2. To add hyperlinks, right-click on the entry point where you wish to place the link, either on a piece of text or an image, and choose Hyperlink from the menu that appears.

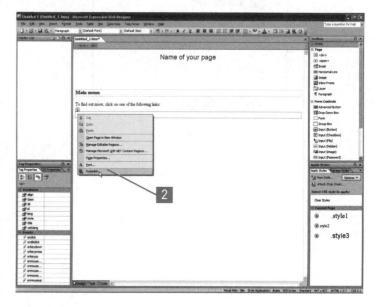

3 Browse to an existing link or page or type in the name of a new page or file that you want to create. You will create a new page or file that will be linked from the main page. If it is an existing page or file then the link is made directly.

4 The page name will appear in the Text to display line but you can change this to what you wish to appear on-screen.

5 Click the ScreenTips link and enter a message in the box that appears. The message you enter will appear in a text window when a visitor to the site hovers their cursor over the link.

Previekwing your pages

Your pages won't look quite the same when viewed through a browser as they do in your Design Space. Make sure you like the result readers will see by previewing your pages.

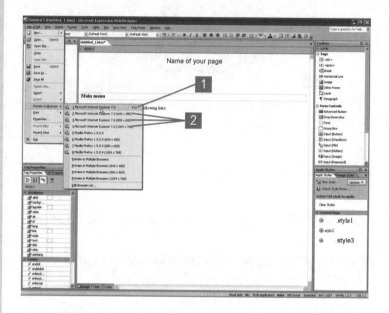

1 You can press the F12 key to quickly preview your page in your default browser – most commonly Internet Explorer.

2 Previewing your page at different resolutions can be useful when checking whether graphics will fit in the window. Remember, not everyone will use the same screen resolution as you.

3 Test all your links and ScreenTips to ensure they work as expected.

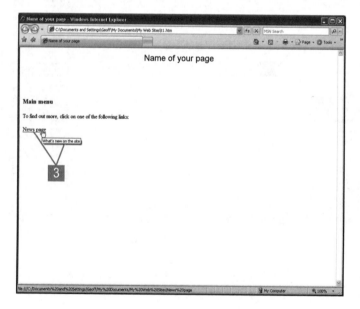

The most popular browser is Internet Explorer which is packaged with Windows XP and Windows Vista operating systems. However, around 20% of PC users are using alternative browsers – Firefox being one of the most popular, with Opera and Safari – a standard browser for Macs – also generating significant followings. Each of them present HTML code slightly differently so it is worth testing your site in the different browsers if you're concerned about the image you're presenting to as wide a range of readers as possible.

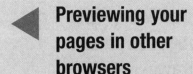

Previewing your pages in other browsers

1 Select Preview in Browser on the File menu.

2 Click on the browser you want to check out and choose an appropriate one. If you can't see the browser you wish to use, click on Edit Browser List.

Previewing your pages in other browsers (cont.)

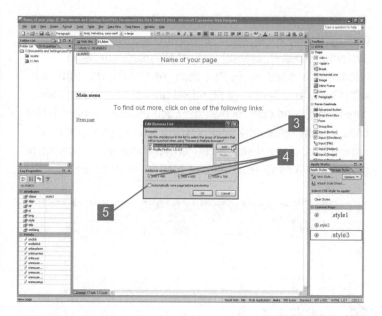

3 Click on Add to add another browser. (Note that you will need to have the browser installed before doing so.) Browse to the directory where your alternative web browsers are filed.

4 If you aren't worried about lower resolutions then you can untick these boxes. The minimum browser window is 800×600 but almost all users have far more desktop space these days thanks to the larger monitors available.

5 As a rule you will want to save your work at every opportunity, so tick this box.

6 Are you happy with the result? Check that the page looks right in the browser and that none of the elements of your page have moved or been realigned.

The Styles tool takes a lot of the hassle out of creating a number of pages for the same site and ensures that you retain a consistent look and feel throughout the site.

Whenever you change a font, its size or style, a new Style is created in the Apply Styles pane. You can quickly apply one of these Styles to any new sections of text to save you formatting them again manually and ensure you don't make minor mistakes that result in numerous slightly different formats. On your first few pages this won't seem immediately useful but as soon as your website expands beyond just a few linked pages, the benefits become clear.

Applying and managing styles

6

1 Enter a new piece of text into the Design Space.

See also

For more information on CSS see Chapter 7 pages 157–161.

Applying and managing styles (cont.)

2. Look at the CSS Styles you have already created in the Apply Styles pane.

3. If you hold the cursor over a style in the Apply Styles pane, you will see the description of the Style appear in a pop-up window.

4. To similarly style another section of text, select it and then click on the Style in the Apply Styles pane.

Timesaver tip

To see all the parts of a page which are designed with a particular CSS Style, right-click on the particular Style and choose Select All Instance(s). There may be a number already in the menu, showing you how many times you have used that style.

Styles really come into their own when you decide that you'd like to change the look and feel of your whole site. If you've used Styles, you can do this very quickly and easily by editing the CSS properties. The new Style will then be applied across all the pages in your project with no laborious re-formatting required.

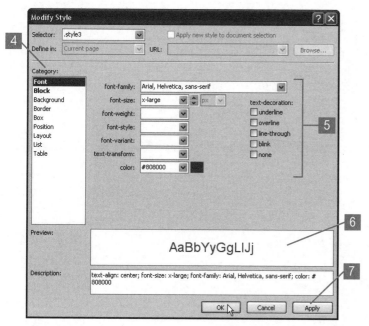

1 Right-click on the style you wish to change in the Apply Styles pane.

2 If you want to create a variant of the existing Style click on New Style Copy to create a duplicate version, allowing you to retain and use the original Style.

3 To change the Style, click Modify Style.

4 You can change different aspects of the Style by selecting from a list of style categories.

5 Customise your style by editing the properties.

6 Preview the changes you have made.

7 Click Apply and OK to accept the changes you are making to the style. The changes will be made and you can see the results in the Design view.

Using layers in Expression

Layers are a common feature in graphics packages like Paint Shop Pro or InDesign. They allow you to place an element in a discrete space, separate from the rest of the document. They can hold text or images and you can make them any size and position them anywhere on the web page. Layers can also be turned on or off so you can see only the elements you need to work on when creating pages.

Layers are at their most useful in Expression when a 'behaviour' is assigned to them. This is a piece of JavaScript code that has an effect on the layer. Preset behaviours that you can select from a list of options include pop-up messages, and images that change in the layer as the cursor passes over them. However, if you can create the JavaScript code almost any behaviour can be incorporated.

1 Go to the Format menu and click Layers.

2 The Layers task pane will appear on the page. It is initially empty and there are two buttons for adding new layers.

3 Click the Insert Layer button and a new layer appears in the Design View.

4 Resize the layer to the right dimensions by clicking and dragging on a corner of the box.

5 Move the layer by holding down the mouse button somewhere inside the box and moving it to the correct position.

6 Right-click on the layer when you're happy with its position and choose the Manage Editable Regions option.

Creating a website using Expression Web Designer 143

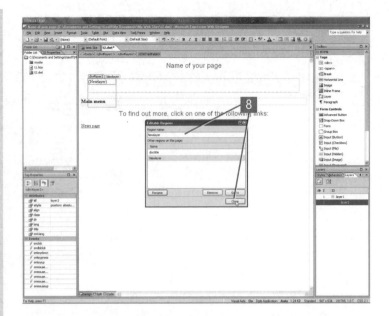

7 You will get a pop-up window telling you that the page must be saved as a Dynamic Web Template to use the feature. Click Yes to save the page as a dynamic template, give it a new name and click OK.

8 The Editable Regions window appears. Give your layer a name and click Close.

9 You can now add content to the layer and change the behaviour using the Format, Behaviour menu.

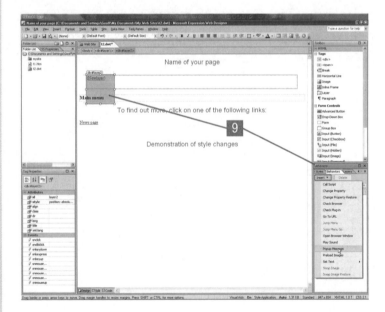

Once you get the hang of writing web pages, you'll want to speed up the process of getting around the Design space. This is where the Quick Command List comes in handy.

1 Go to the Help menu, at the top right of the screen or press F1.

2 Type 'Quick Command List' into the search box. Click on Search.

3 Click on Keyboard Shortcuts link.

4 The command list shows shortcut keys to some common functions like text formatting to program specific features such as Code view and web page shortcuts.

5 Scroll down the list to find specific sections of advice.

Creating a website using Expression Web Designer 145

Shortcuts reference list

Web page shortcuts

To do this	Press
Create a new web page.	CTRL+N
Open a web page.	CTRL+O
Close a web page.	CTRL+F4
Save a web page.	CTRL+S
Print a web page.	CTRL+P
Refresh a web page or refresh **Code** view changes in **Design** view.	F5
Switch between open web pages.	CTRL+TAB
Switch between open web pages in reverse order.	CTRL+SHIFT +TAB
Preview a web page in a web browser.	F12 or CTRL+SHIFT+B
Delete a web page or folder in the **Folder List** task pane or any dialog box.	DELETE
Move between **Code**, **Design**, and **Split** views.	CTRL+PAGE DOWN or CTRL+PAGE UP
Move between **Code** and **Design** panes in **Split** view.	ALT+PAGE DOWN or ALT+PAGE UP
Show or hide the **Folder List** task pane.	ALT+F1
Rename the currently selected file in the **Folder List** task pane.	F2

Application shortcuts

To do this	Press
Quit Expression Web.	ALT+F4
Cancel an action.	ESC
Undo an action.	CTRL+Z or ALT+ BACKSPACE
Redo or repeat an action.	CTRL+Y or SHIFT+ALT+ BACKSPACE
Toggle between open dialog boxes.	ALT+F6
Toggle between open dialog boxes in reverse order.	ALT+SHIFT+F6

Find and replace shortcuts

To do this	Press
Find text or code.	CTRL+F
Find the next occurrence of the most recent search.	F3
Find the previous occurrence of the most recent search.	SHIFT+F3
Find the next occurrence of the current selection.	CTRL+F3
Find the previous occurrence of the current selection.	CTRL+SHIFT+F3
Replace text or code.	CTRL+H
Check spelling.	F7
Look up a word in the thesaurus.	SHIFT+F7

Code view shortcuts

To do this	Press
Quick tag editor.	CTRL+Q
Insert temporary bookmark.	CTRL+F2
Next temporary bookmark.	F2
Previous temporary bookmark.	SHIFT+F2
Go to line.	CTRL+G
Insert code snippet.	CTRL+ENTER
Insert end tag.	CTRL+.
Insert start tag.	CTRL+,
Insert HTML comment.	CTRL+/
Complete word.	CTRL+ SPACEBAR
Select tag and its contents.	CTRL+SHIFT+:
Find matching tag.	CTRL+;
Perform an incremental search.	CTRL+ALT+F

Text shortcuts

To do this	Press
Apply bold formatting.	CTRL+B
Apply an underline.	CTRL+U
Apply italic formatting.	CTRL+I
Apply superscript formatting.	CTRL+PLUS SIGN
Apply subscript formatting.	CTRL+EQUAL SIGN
Copy text or graphics.	CTRL+C or CTRL+INSERT
Cut selected text or graphics.	CTRL+X or SHIFT+DELETE
Paste text or graphics.	CTRL+V or SHIFT+INSERT
Copy formatting.	CTRL+ SHIFT+C
Paste formatting.	CTRL+SHIFT+V
Remove manual formatting.	CTRL+SHIFT+Z or CTRL+SPACEBAR
Center a paragraph.	CTRL+E
Left align a paragraph.	CTRL+L
Right align a paragraph.	CTRL+R
Indent a paragraph from the left.	CTRL+M
Indent a paragraph from the right.	CTRL+ SHIFT+M
Insert a line break.	SHIFT+ENTER
Insert a nonbreaking space.	CTRL+SHIFT+ SPACEBAR

Tables, graphics, and hyperlinks shortcuts

To do this	Press
Insert a table.	SHIFT+CTRL+ ALT+T
Select the next table cell's content.	TAB
Select the preceding table cell's content.	SHIFT+TAB
With a graphic selected, create an auto thumbnail.	CTRL +T
Create a hyperlink on a web page.	CTRL+K

Advanced techniques

Introduction

Now that you've seen how to create a website and then populate it with all of the content necessary to make your project appealing to potential visitors, it's time to take a look at some advanced techniques that will make your site look professional and operate even more efficiently. We will demonstrate these techniques using FrontPage, but Expression Web contains the same tools.

What you'll do

Explore Frames

Use tables

Discover cascading style sheets

Benefit from our web usability design tips

Exploring Frames

The Frames tools give you much more control over the way your web pages look and behave. They enable you to create a more ordered, well structured and easily navigable site. Using Frames, you can effectively create two or more web pages that are displayed as one. For example, a page containing two frames can consist of a navigation frame that remains in place even when the buttons are activated, and a content frame that changes in response to the user's clicks.

1 Select File, New.

2 Click on the Frames Pages tab. This displays a variety of framesets for you to choose from. Note the description and the preview on the right-hand side.

3 Select a frameset and it opens in the workspace. You will see that the two frames are clearly defined and can be worked on independently. The frameset we have chosen will be ideal for a navigation menu (narrower, left-hand frame) and associated content pages (larger, right-hand frame).

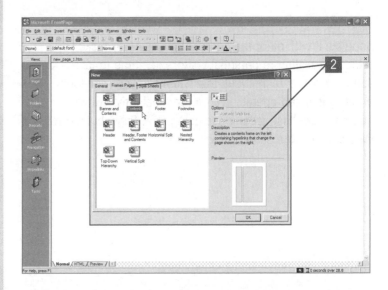

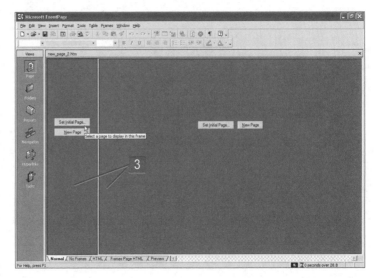

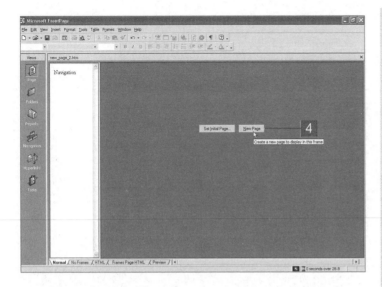

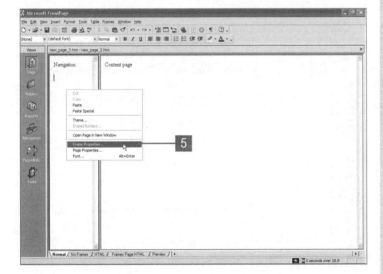

4 Each area of your frameset will initially have the same options. Click on New Page to create a page from scratch.

5 Format your new page quickly and easily by right clicking within the page and selecting Frame Properties… from the menu.

7

Timesaver tip

The dividing line or margin between the two frames is moveable so you can resize your frames simply by clicking and dragging it one way or the other.

See also

See pages 142–144 in Chapter 6 to find out how to employ layers to create advanced features on your website using Expression Web.

Exploring Frames (cont.)

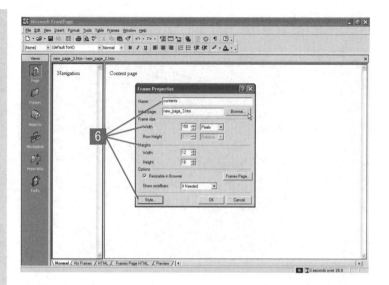

6 Give your page an appropriate name. Select values for your frame size and margins if you wish to amend the frameset template and move on to select your Styles.

7 Content and graphics can be cut and pasted or inserted into the frame as described in Chapter 4.

8 Alternatively, right click on your frame again and select Theme… to take advantage of a range of different designs that you can populate with your own content.

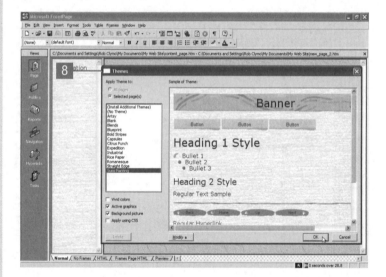

Timesaver tip

Planning is everything in the world of web design and it's a really good idea to sketch out a map of the pages you wish to incorporate into your frameset. This will ensure that everything ends up linking together successfully and you won't tie yourself up in knots!

For your information

Notice that FrontPage has a few more tabs along the bottom of the main workspace now that you are working with Frames. By clicking on the HTML option you can see that the frames are essentially two separate web pages with their own HTML code, working in tandem due to the frameset structure.

Timesaver tip

Make a note of any specific themes, colour schemes or typefaces that you use in one frame within a frameset so that you can match them to the other frames. Otherwise you can end up with a curious mish-mash of styles that detract from the content of your site.

7

Important

Although undoubtedly a powerful and useful tool, Frames should be used sparingly – keep the structure simple. Some older browsers cannot view them properly and some search engines don't reference them properly.

Important

One of the most important things to remember when using Frames is to save all of your pages and other content in the same root folder. This is because framesets involve making lots of pages and content link together in order to work.

Using tables

If you are having trouble positioning your content correctly on the web page and maintaining the same format across different pages, you will find the Tables feature useful.

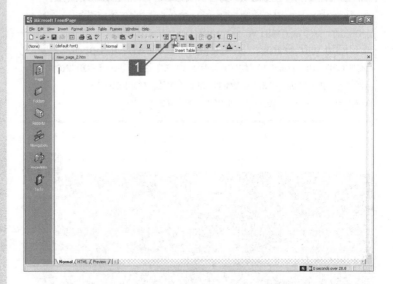

1 Select Insert Table from the main toolbar (or use the Table menu).

2 Chose the number of rows and columns you require.

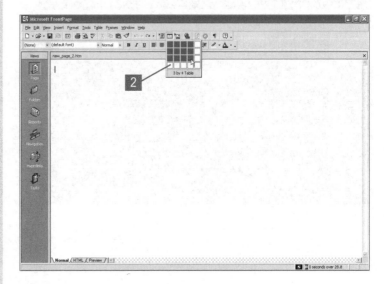

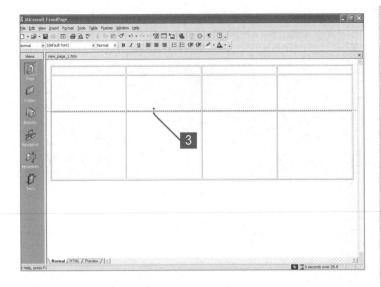

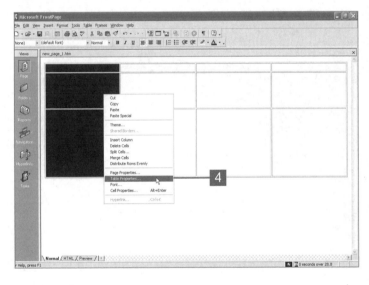

3 Change the table's and cells' dimensions if necessary.

4 Right click on the page and select Table Properties... to select styles for borders, backgrounds, etc. If you want your table to fill the browser window, select the width and height to be 100 percent. Alternatively make your table a fixed size.

7

Using tables (cont.)

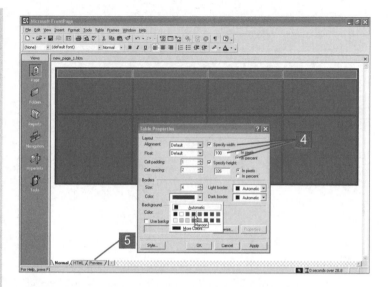

5 Click on the Preview tab at the foot of the page to see how your design is shaping up.

6 Insert text, graphics (remember to pre-size them so they fit) and hyperlinks into individual cells and when everything is complete, you can hide the borders to disguise the fact that it is a table at all.

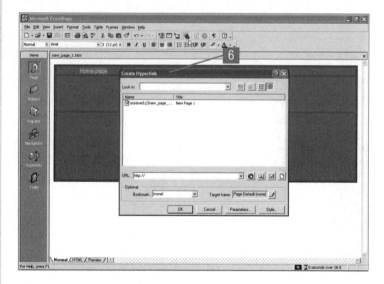

Another great way of exercising more control over the way your website looks when viewed by a variety of users is to employ Cascading Style Sheets (CSS). There are three ways you can incorporate CSS in your web pages. Firstly you can reference an external document (.css file) containing all the style information to be applied to a website or set of pages. An organisation might make use of this to ensure all the websites in its jurisdiction conform. Alternatively, the styles can be embedded in the HTML document itself. In this case they are included in the HEAD section of the code to apply to an entire page. And finally inline styles modify the HTML tag for a single element and are applied using the Style tools.

Discovering cascading style sheets

1 To create a new style select Format, Style…

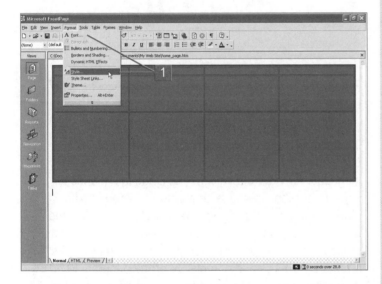

Important

Whilst using the power of CSS can transform the way you design a web page remember that it is crucial you stick to the basic rules of design. Just because you *can* create luminescent blinking text on your page doesn't necessarily means that you *should*.

Discovering cascading style sheets (cont.)

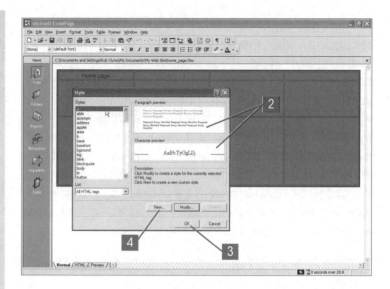

2 The Style dialog box contains a lot of preset options so you don't have to re-invent the wheel. Check the preview on the right-hand side to see what each style does.

3 Click OK if you're happy with using one of the preset Styles.

4 Alternatively, select New to create your own Style.

Jargon buster

CSS – short for Cascading Style Sheets – a style sheet language that is used to define the presentation of documents where the content is written in a mark up language, for example, HTML. The language defines all aspects of presentation such as fonts, colours, text sizes, layout, etc. The key feature of CSS is that in using it, you can separate the content of the web page from its presentation. This powerful tool has numerous benefits: it reduces the size and complexity of the document code by removing all the presentational elements, it provides the website designer with a very quick and easy way to change the style of an entire website in a matter or clicks, it even allows the reader to change the way the content is presented to suit his/her needs (e.g. changing the layout to suit a smaller screen on a mobile phone).

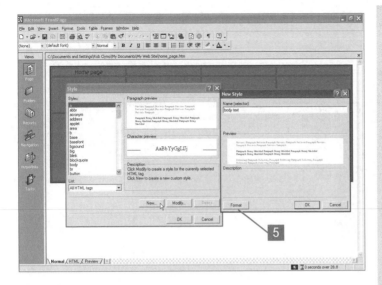

5 The New Style dialog box provides all the different formatting options you will need. Click on Format.

6 We'll work on the font of our body text.

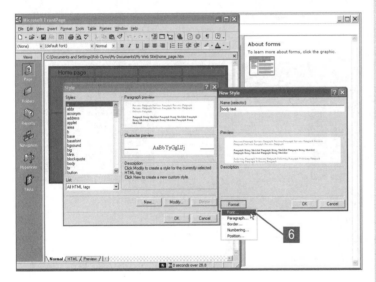

Discovering cascading style sheets (cont.)

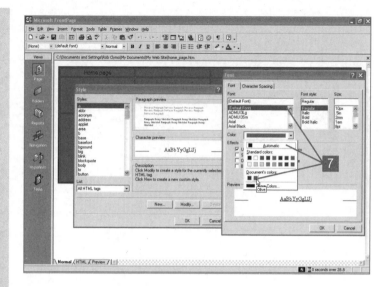

7 Select the font, its colour and characteristics. Note that along with the standard web-safe colour palette, FrontPage also shows you the colours that already exist in your document helping you to avoid incorporating too many similar or clashing shades.

8 Click OK and then save the Style using an appropriate name in the User-defined styles list. Click OK to apply.

9 Use the three different management buttons at the bottom of the Style dialog box to create, modify or delete CSS files as and when you need to.

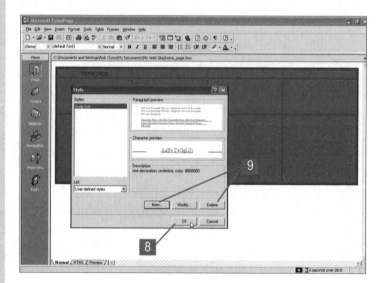

Important

If you are linking to an external style sheet then it is a good idea to save this inside your root folder to avoid any problems when you upload your files to the web.

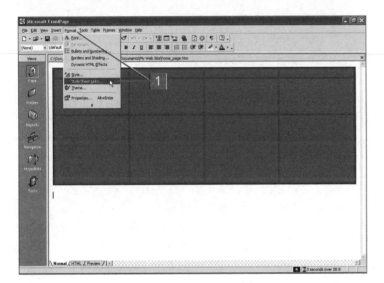

Linking to an external CSS file

1 Select Format, Style Sheet Links... and type in the name of the file you want your page to link to.

7

Web usability design tips

Contributed by Lon Barfield, Usability Design Partnership

Be understood

Draw up a list of standard terms

Terminology needs to be defined and consistently used.

A website is usually set up to deal with one topic. That topic will doubtless involve many new concepts and terms. Before starting to write the text, or before importing or repurposing text from other publishing streams, you should decide on how the key concepts are going to be named.

The best way to approach this on a practical level is to draw up a list of concepts with temporary names (since you have to call them something while you are discussing what to call them!), put it in a spreadsheet and then arrange a couple of meetings with stake holders and users to decide which ones to use. Bear in mind that you really need to be in touch with what the user will call the things and that you have to get approval to use the terms you choose if there is a formal organisation behind the website.

This process should be applied not only to the terminology related to the content of the website but also to the terminology related to the use of the website itself. For example is it 'home page', 'start' or 'home'? Is it 'visitors' favourites' or 'hot topics'?

Speak the user's language

Make sure that the terms you use in your website are the same ones your intended audience are going to be using.

Visitors to a website will find it easier to use if it speaks the same language as they do. It is all too easy for a website designer to use language that is quite specific to a particular organisation or interest group. This can result in a website that is completely comprehensible to the designer, but ambiguous to end users. Exclusive terminology can easily creep in during the website development process so audit all terminology before finalising your text.

For example, in a public facing website about current world health risks don't have a section on 'avian influenza', call it 'bird flu' instead.

Don't be too zealous

People usually use the web for information. They want to get to information quickly and then do something else. They are not interested if you think that what you are offering is the best thing ever invented – they want the information so that *they* can decide if it is the best thing ever invented.

If you, or someone in your organisation, really feels that they have to use exciting but obscure terms then make sure that those terms are qualified with explanatory text. If a term is not explained and not known to the user, they will simply move on to another, more useful, website.

So don't say 'Super Blogomatic', instead say 'Super Blogomatic – the automatic blogging tool that creates a blog framework for you from your email in-box'.

Make it easy to identify links

Links are a vital part of any website. Make sure the user can tell what are links and what are not.

You need to adopt a consistent link style so that users quickly become accustomed to navigating around your site. If the link style is consistent across your site then users will get the hang of it and be able to use the site without difficulty. You can choose to use a certain colour for links and maybe a certain text style. Make sure though that the link style does not clash with any other styles in the website. Ideally styles should complement each other so that they can be combined sensibly – if a heading is also a link you can make it look like both. Better still make the link style consistent with that used on the rest of the web – this ensures that users will be familiar with how the links work as soon as they come to your site.

Don't make pages jump about

Keep navigation and page layout as consistent as possible.

For your information

Users are generally used to link text being blue and underlined, turning to purple once the linked-to site has been visited. Most of the big players go along with this and other sites pay homage to it with slight variations in colours.

7

Ever had someone clear up your kitchen for you and put everything back in the wrong place? We like to have things in the same place each time and this is true for websites as well. Users find it easier if one screen is similar to another. They acquire a feeling of familiarity and they don't have to relearn the interface with each screen they see. Throughout the website, buttons and links should stay in similar positions within the window, not jump about around the screen.

Furthermore their positions should not be dependent upon the extent of the content in a page. For example, it's not a good idea to position 'previous' and 'next' buttons at the bottom of a paragraph of text, where that paragraph is one of a series of similar paragraphs on subsequent pages. If you do, the buttons will migrate up and down the screen as the user clicks from one page to the next, resulting in the user having to continually reposition their mouse.

Be very wary of icons

Graphic designers can get carried away with icons, but icons alone are not a guarantee of usability.

Some designers love icons. Rather than spend time on page layout they will happily spend ages designing and tweaking ranges of obscure icons for every conceivable component of the site. Similarly, website creation applications like the ones described in this book often have galleries of icons that you can choose to pepper your pages with.

Just having icons in a web page is no guarantee of usability. Often the reverse is true – everyone can understand the text: 'read only file', but if you have a minute picture of a funny looking folder with a pair of glasses next to it, the user could be understandably confused.

If you have an uncontrollable urge to use icons, try to use standard ones and only design new ones if you are going to carry out proper user tests. Showing a group of users a range of icons and having them say 'I have no idea what these mean' is one of the key ways to identify gratuitous icon usage.

Avoid text in image form

Text in a web page can be embedded in HTML code or in an image. The former is better.

If you include text as an image (i.e. in a graphics file) then you might expect that most visitors to the site will be able to read it. However, there are visitors that won't be able to, in particular automatic search engine indexers and people with impaired vision. The former are software programs that run night and day calling up sites and automatically indexing the content. They do this by processing the text in the page. If the text is part of an image they cannot access it, to them it is just an image. So, if you have important text in an image at the top of your page then make sure the text is also included as normal text in a high profile part of the page. Alternatively put it in the ALT tag of the image the search engine indexers can access this.

Vision impaired users rely on a screen reader to 'read' web pages. This screen reader is a software application like a search engine indexer, except that it reads the words out loud so that the user can hear what the page is about. Once again if the text is contained in an image this program won't be able to access it.

For your information

Interestingly enough there may be times when you want to hide bits of text so that automatic systems can't read them. For example, if you are including an email address on the website. Some unscrupulous automatic programs browse the web searching and gathering email addresses to send junk email to. If your email address is embedded in an image these sorts of programs will not be able to decipher it while a human visitor to the page will.

Group related items

When you sort out your desk, do you clear every single bit of junk and scrap of paper away? Of course not! You tidy it up by piling things together and clustering them; all the financial letters get piled up in that corner, the bits of things that need fixing are all laid out here, important stuff is in the little pile right at the front of the desk, photos are in two piles at the back, etc. When things are grouped together like this it means that instead of having to think about lots of small items you just have to think about the clusters. All the items are still there, but they are made more manageable by the groupings.

The same is true when it comes to items that are distributed around a web page, in particular the navigational links. In some websites there are literally hundreds of them per page. While you should do all you can to keep them to a minimum, you can still end up with loads on display and the best way to make them more manageable is to group them together in logical ways.

You can group by function, scope, frequency of use, etc. And you can gather them together under headings that explain them and explicitly associate them.

Use high contrast between text and background

If you are using dark text use it in combination with a light background and vice versa.

Dark text on a light background or light text on a dark background is easier to read than text that is distinguished from the background only by its colour. The greater the difference in light and dark the more readable the text will be. This is because, when the eye perceives light and dark, it is very good at picking out boundaries. But when the eye perceives different colours, the boundaries look blurred.

This is especially true when using the colour blue because the eye reacts to blue light in a different way to other colours. Blue is often used as the colour for links because it has become something of a standard throughout the web. So, if you are following this standard then use dark blue against a light background or very light blue against a dark background.

For your information

There is plenty of design advice available on the web. Sometimes looking at how NOT to do it is a useful strategy. Head to the humorous 'Web Pages That Suck' site at www.webpagesthatsuck.com or to www.shockingsites.co.uk. And if you'd like to see how to do it properly, visit Jakob Nielsen's website at www.useit.com for some great guidelines or to www.killersites.com.

Web usability design tips (cont.)

Position important stuff in the top left section of the page

Items at the top of a page are perceived as more important than those near the bottom, and items at the left of the page are perceived as more important that those on the right.

In the West we read from left to right and from top to bottom, so our eye is drawn to the top left when 'reading' a screen. Also, this is where the important initial bits of information are: titles are at the top; heading numbering is on the left; numbered items run top to bottom or left to right; etc.

When you are designing the layout for a page, make sure that you put the key items at the left and towards the top: company logos; home page button; etc. Put less important, more contextual stuff to the right: help buttons; etc. And put links to background information at the bottom of the page: terms and conditions; copyright notices; etc.

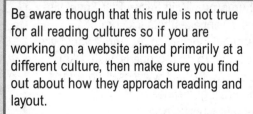

For your information

Be aware though that this rule is not true for all reading cultures so if you are working on a website aimed primarily at a different culture, then make sure you find out about how they approach reading and layout.

Only use animation when appropriate

Don't make things move on a website unless having them move will, in some way, be useful to the user.

The eye is drawn very easily to movement. This is true in the natural world and it remains true in website design. If part of your page is moving or jiggling or flashing, then the user's eye will continually be drawn towards it.

Such tricks are usually included by designers who think that it looks cool to have flashy features or by technicians who feel that they have to show off their programming skills.

Avoid long lines of text

Lines longer than 15 words make reading paragraphs more difficult.

When you are designing the layout of large amounts of text, make sure that you have well defined widths for the text areas. If the width of the text area is purely dependent upon the width of the window then the legibility of the text depends upon the size of the user's window, which is often too wide. The optimal number of words per line is between 10 and 12 with 15 as a maximum.

Use tables or, better still, use cascading style sheets to limit the maximum width of the text areas.

Keep text short and scan-able

There is nothing worse than a long, long page of text that you have to scroll through endlessly.

The web is not read in the same way as printed matter. The closest medium is the newspaper. Text should contain short paragraphs and should be written in an inverted pyramid style. Start with a summary and then gradually expand upon it.

The text on the web page can be made more scan-able and easy to navigate by splitting it up with headings, sub-headings, boxed elements, quotations and images. Bear in mind though that it is not good to include these elements purely to split the text up. Make sure that these extra elements are relevant.

Important

If you want your site to be viewed as widely as possible, make sure you take the needs of visually impaired users and those with disabilities into account. Find out about design tips and technology you can employ at the Web Accessibility Initiative located at www.w3.org/WAI.

7

Getting online

Introduction

The prerequisite for this chapter is that you have a fully functioning website now working smoothly on your own PC. You've checked to see how different browsers handle the styles and features you have included, and that all the links work. Now you need to get it online so that all the world can view the fruits of your labours. In this chapter we will demonstrate how to find an Internet Service Provider (ISP) to host your site, how to register your own personal domain name, how to upload your files to the server and, finally, how to use 3rd party internet services to test and optimise your site.

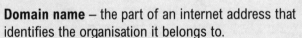

Jargon buster

Domain name – the part of an internet address that identifies the organisation it belongs to.

What you'll do

Find an ISP to host your site

Use a web hosting provider

Buy a domain name

Get help from Nominet

Use FTP software to connect to your site

Upload your files via FTP

Test your website

Find an ISP to host your site

The first place to look for server space for your website is your own ISP – the company that you subscribe to provide your dial-up or broadband internet connection. Most ISPs include a certain amount of server space for free with their connection package – so check on the home page of your provider to see what kind of allowance you have already got.

1 We will use Orange in this example, but you are likely to find the relevant information in similar sections of your own ISP's website. Navigate to the 'my account' section of the website where you will be asked to login.

2 The member centre contains a link to a 'Build a website' section which contains information about the storage space you are entitled to as well as links to proprietary online site building services and information on how to buy a domain name.

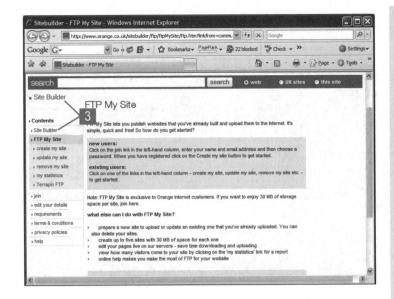

3 The Site Builder option contains information on how to upload your site to the Orange server using File Transfer Protocol (FTP).

Jargon buster

FTP – short for File Transfer Protocol – the method most usually used for transferring files across the internet.

Server – a computer that provides services to other computers. A web server is a remote computer with which your computer communicates in order to access websites. Billions of servers house the data and information on the web.

8

Find an ISP to host your site (cont.)

4 Of course, if you have used an online web building service such as ZyWeb and WebEden as described in Chapter 3, the hosting is provided as part of the package.

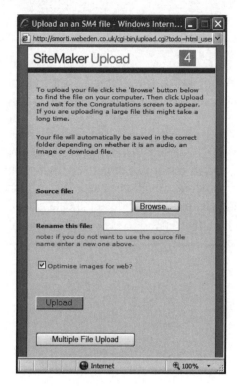

If you need more space than your ISP can provide, there are plenty of alternative web hosting providers to check out.

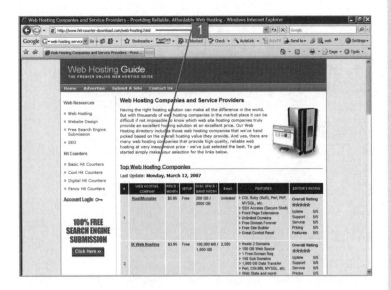

1. If you need to use an independent web hosting provider for any reason, you'll find a useful directory here.

2. 1&1 Internet is fairly typical and has packages to suit every pocket.

8

Important

Make sure that you do not send credit or debit card information over the internet unless the website has a secure system in place. Look out for that little padlock in the toolbar of your browser.

Using a web hosting provider (cont.)

3 To get a better understanding of what the different packages feature it's worth spending some time looking at the information on each. The Home package would be suitable for most personal websites.

4 This web hosting provider also allows you to buy a domain name at the same time and build it into the overall price. Some domain names come free if you sign up for hosting.

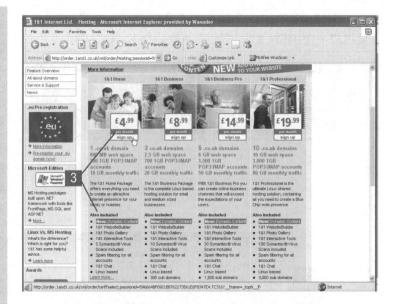

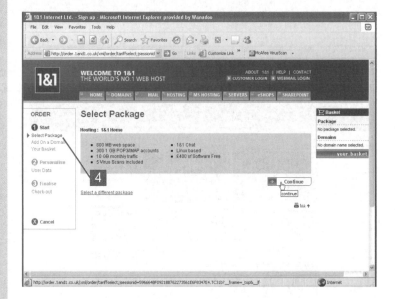

Timesaver tip

Make a note of the host name for your site, your user name and password. You'll need this information when it comes to uploading your files.

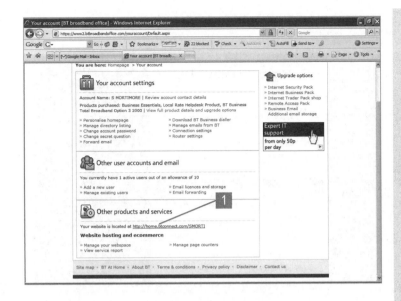

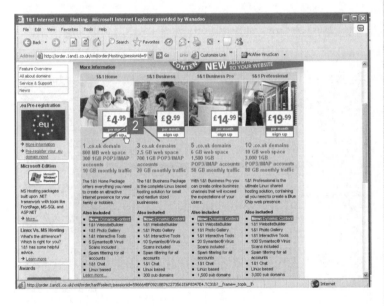

Buying a domain name

1 If you have used your ISP to host your website, you will probably have a free domain name (or more) included in your package. The only drawback is that your unique identifier is added to their corporate domain name so it doesn't look as personal as you might like.

2 Alternatively, your web hosting provider may have thrown in a free domain name or two with your package.

8

Buying a domain name (cont.)

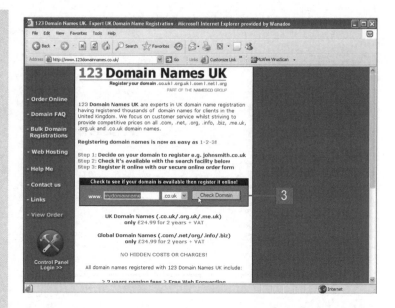

3 If you'd prefer to use an independent service, there are many to be found by typing 'Domain names' into Google. 123 Domain Names UK is a fairly typical service. The first thing you have to do is check to see if your preferred name is still available.

4 The search will bring up a list of the variants that are available and how much registration will cost.

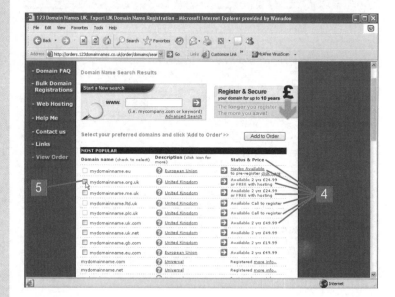

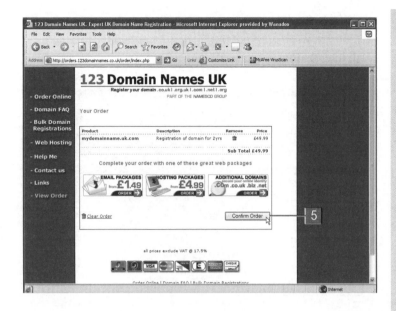

5 Click on the check box by the name you chose and follow the registration instructions.

For your information

You'll note that there are many different extensions available for you to add to your domain name: .co.uk is the most common for UK-based companies but also possible are: .org.uk, .eu and .com. For a personal site you may chose a .me.uk extension and .info for a hobby or pastime site. You can't just make up the extension though – the extensions available are specified by the International Internet Registries.

8

Important

Note that you register a domain name for a fixed time period – most frequently 2 years. You will be sent a bill for your renewal fee when the registration expires.

Getting help from Nominet

Nominet is the Internet Registry for .uk domain names. It can be found at www.nominet.org.uk and it contains a complete list of all the .uk domain names.

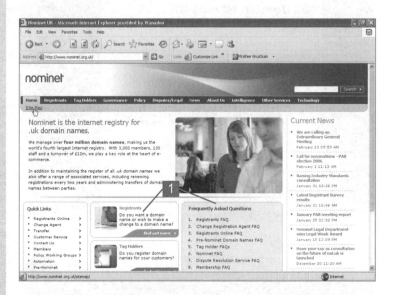

1. This is a great place to visit if you are unsure of the steps involved in getting a domain name or if you have encountered problems along the way. Nominet can also help resolve any disputes that may occur over ownership of domain names.

2. There is a useful list of Frequently Asked Questions (FAQs) which will answer just about any query you may have relating to a domain name registered here in the UK.

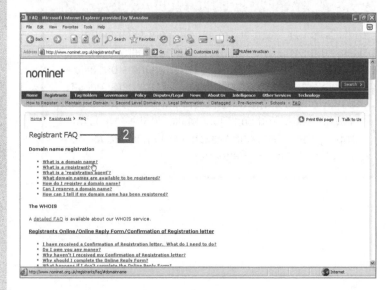

Jargon buster

FAQs – Frequently Asked Questions – a list of the most common questions users of a website may pose. Referring to this section of the site is the first port of call if you don't understand something about the way it functions.

If you've used an online service such as ZyWeb or WebEden, your website is automatically uploaded to the internet when you publish it. However, if your files are currently sitting on your PC and awaiting transfer to your newly registered web domain, you need to know about File Transfer Protocol (FTP). It is not complicated and you can get software especially designed to handle it – FTP is essentially just a way of copying files from your PC to a remote one, usually called a web server.

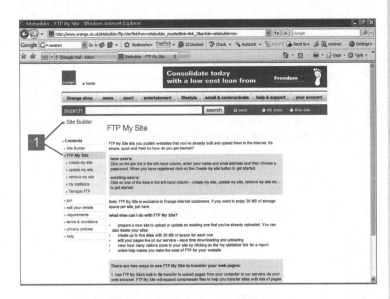

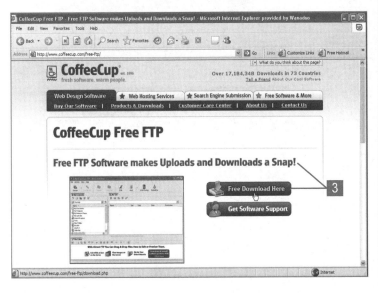

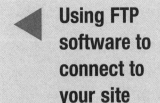

Using FTP software to connect to your site

1 Many ISPs include FTP software with their web hosting and site building packages.

2 FrontPage and ExpressionWeb contain an integral FTP toolset which makes uploading your files very straightforward.

3 There are also lots of website builder and FTP software companies that provide versions of their package for free. CoffeeCup is one of these. It doesn't take long to register and download the software to your PC.

8

Using FTP software to connect to your site (cont.)

4 When it first launches, the CoffeeCup FTP program shows this dialog box. Click on Add and you will be taken through the set-up by a Server Profile Wizard.

5 In the future you may have numerous remote sites you wish to connect to and these will be listed under My Sites, so give this one a name that reflects what it is. Click on Next.

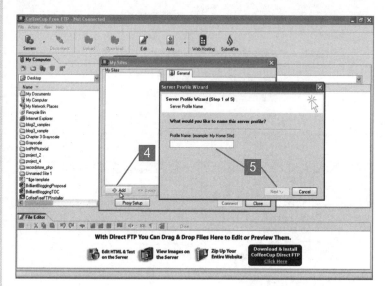

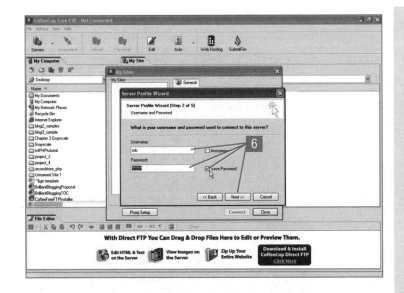

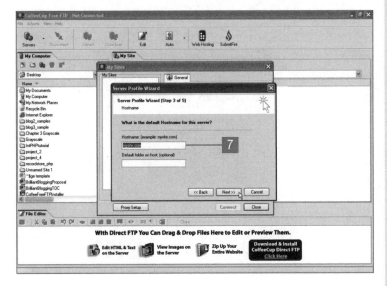

6 Enter the user name and password you were provided with by your web hosting provider or ISP. You can also check the Save Password option so it'll be automatically entered next time you log in. Click Next.

7 The server name should also have been provided by your web hosting provider or ISP. If not, one of the best places to look for it is on your ISP's or web host's website FAQ pages.

8

Using FTP software to connect to your site (cont.)

8 You will know if you are using a proxy server!

9 The server setup is completed. Click Finish.

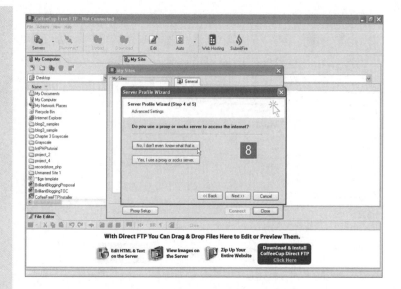

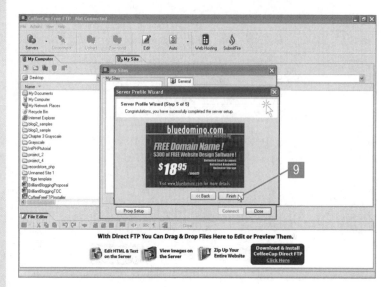

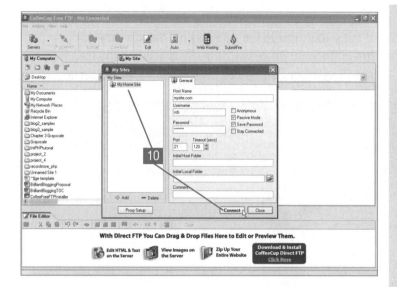

10 You will see that all the relevant information has been incorporated into the My Sites dialog box and all you need to do is click Connect. In future, you just need to double click on the server profile name you provided at the beginning which is now listed under My Sites on the left-hand side, and you'll automatically be connected.

8

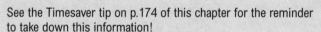

See also

See the Timesaver tip on p.174 of this chapter for the reminder to take down this information!

Uploading your files via FTP

After making a connection to the web server you are then free to copy your files to the web space. This is a very straightforward process that involves sending the files, including images and other page elements, to the server.

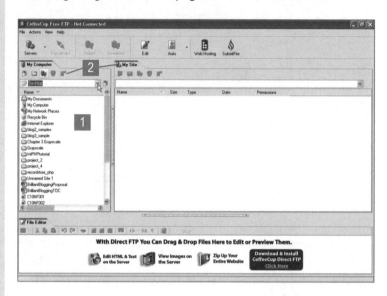

1. Take a few moments to familiarise yourself with the interface. The screen is divided into two. You can see the files on your own PC listed on the left. The files you transfer will be listed on the right.

2. Use the tools in the My Computer and My Site toolbars to move the files around just as you would in most file management systems. The main thing to remember is that you are moving them to a remote computer, so you need to remain connected and be patient if things take a little longer than normal.

Important

Occasionally, your connection may break. If this happens, just click on the Reconnect button in the toolbar and restart from where you left off.

For your information

CoffeCup Free FTP software is ideal for moving a small number of files around. But if you have a lot of files and you update them quite frequently, you will find the more sophisticated FTP functions in some of the web authoring tools that are available, like Dreamweaver or NetObjects, more powerful.

Did you know?

Visitors are much more likely to come back to view your site if they think there will be something new to see. In that respect it's a good idea to include a 'page/site last updated' indicator, along with a date which will allow people to see how recently the page was modified.

Once your site is online, it is worth making sure it operates as it should. There are some tools available to help you with this.

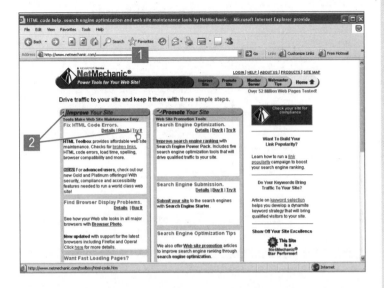

1 NetMechanic is an online optimisation service that allows you to check up to five pages for free. Go to www.netmechanic.com and spend some time exploring the array of options for improving the durability of your website.

2 We'll start with the 'Improve Your Site' option that will check for HTML code errors, broken links and typos as well as download times and browser compatibility. Click on the Try It link.

3 Scroll down to find the HTML Toolbox Free Sample.

8

Testing your
website (cont.)

4 Enter the URL of your site and the number of pages you'd like to check. You will need to enter your email address and click Test Now.

5 You will see a progress indicator showing you how many tests are being carried out.

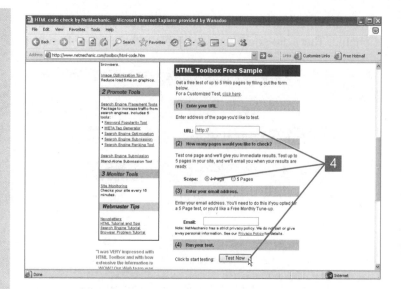

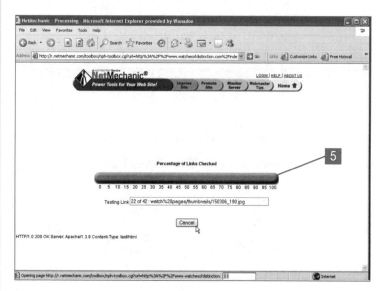

See also

We will cover ways to promote your site in Chapter 9.

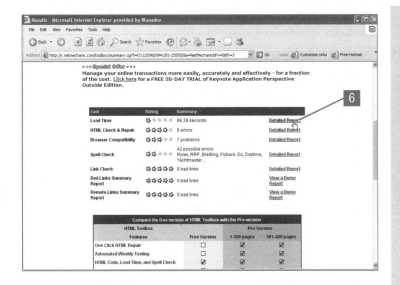

6 Your results. Click on the Detailed Report links for more information. And of course, note that the Pro Version will do much more if you choose to shell out.

Important

If you find that some of your links don't work when you try them from your website – and they did work when you tested them on your computer – check the case of the filenames. If you have a link to 'Tiddles.htm' and the file was called 'tiddles.htm' the link may not work. Some FTP tools are case-sensitive in the way they handle filenames.

For your information

There are quite a lot of these online tools that aid the optimisation and testing of websites. However, many of them are paid for services. If you are not sure where to look then try typing something like 'Free web site optimisation' into a search engine like Google and spend a little time checking out the numerous results.

8

Getting your site seen

Introduction

There's no doubting that the web has made it easier for us to make ourselves, our views and our products known to others. However, the sheer amount of information on the internet makes it very easy to remain in obscurity if you don't do something to make your site different from the crowd. In this chapter we'll take you through some web-savvy techniques for getting your site noticed. However, none of these can replace good old fashioned marketing. Promoting your site in print media and by word of mouth is absolutely vital if you are aiming for significant numbers of visitors.

Timesaver tip

Don't forget to promote your website yourself wherever you can. A quick, easy and free way of doing this is to add the URL and a short description to your email signature.

Adding keywords and descriptions in a META tag

This task demonstrates how the HTML META tag is coded so that even if you are using a program like FrontPage where you don't have to do the coding (see the next task), you can understand how the HTML is structured. The META tag allows you to add information about a page, for use by search engines and directories when they add the page to their databases. On a personal website, it would only be written into the index page, and would refer to the whole site. On larger sites you could include META tags for each page if the variety of content deems it necessary.

> **Jargon buster**
>
> **Meta data** – information written into the header section of HTML documents for the benefit of automatic software applications such as web crawlers that visit and read websites, but that is not visible on screen.

The basic META tag shape is:

    <META NAME = …CONTENT = ….>

The NAME can be a range of things including:

- keywords, for indexing by search engines
- description, which some search engines and directories will use when listing your site.

The CONTENT is any appropriate text. For keywords it can be a series of words or 'phrases in double quotation marks', separated by commas, e.g. if someone used their site to organise and advertise their local pigeon fancying club, the index page should have a tag like this:

    <META NAME = keywords CONTENT = 'racing pigeons',
    'Grimsby Feathers Club', Humberside, races, birds>

190

Timesaver tip

Compile a list of keywords as you build your website and make sure that they reflect the content. Be clear and concise.

```
<HTML>
<HEAD>
<META NAME = keywords CONTENT = Clymo, "Pearson
Education", HTML, "web pages", samples, brilliant>
<META NAME = description CONTENT = "Sample web page files
from Brilliant Create your own Website">
<TITLE>Mac's web site at Wanadoo</TITLE>
</HEAD>

<BODY>
....
```

Jargon buster

Keywords – a hand-picked set of words that have relevance to a particular website. Used by automatic search engines to determine which pages match the user's search criteria.

Adding keywords and descriptions in a META tag (cont.)

1. Open your index.htm file.

2. Add two new lines into the HEAD area, and type in the <META... tags for the keywords and description. Follow the structure shown here, but with your own content.

3. Save the file.

4. Open the file in Internet Explorer. You should not see any change at all – if there is something different, there must be something very wrong with one or other of the new tags!

9

Inserting keywords and descriptions using Expression Web

By using Expression Web (or FrontPage), you don't have to do the coding yourself, but you still need to know where to insert the tags – i.e. in the HEAD section of the HTML.

1 Click on the code tab at the bottom of the screen to open Code view.

2 Have the Toolbox task pane open, select HTML and drag the META tag to the position that you want it in your code.

OR

Place your cursor in the position you want the tag to go. In the Insert menu, select HTML and click on the META tag.

You will have to insert the content of the keyword and description tags yourself of course – see the preceding task.

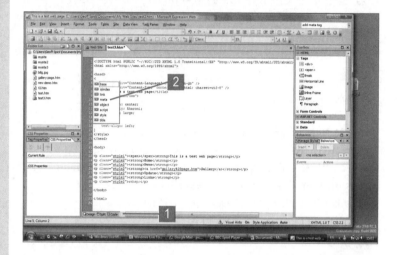

Timesaver tip

If you want all new visitors to be directed to your home page first, then the keywords should be added to the HEAD section of that page. However, if visitors will be better served by being linked directly to the relevant page of your site, include different keywords and descriptions in the META tags of individual pages. You can copy and paste META tags from one page to another so you don't have to enter any common data more than once.

Did you know?

You can of course actually add misspelt keywords in order to catch visitors who have inadvertently spelt a word they are looking for incorrectly.

Did you know?

As you might expect, there are many online services that can help you produce content for the HEAD section of your pages. Type 'Meta Tags Generator' into a search engine to see what is available.

It is very definitely worth submitting information about your site to the major search engines. There are numerous options available to you when it comes to do doing this. You can manually submit your site, which gives you much greater power over which engines you submit your content to. Alternatively, you can use site submission software that enables you to submit information to multiple search engines. The downside of the latter is that it can occasionally lead to you being bombarded by spam.

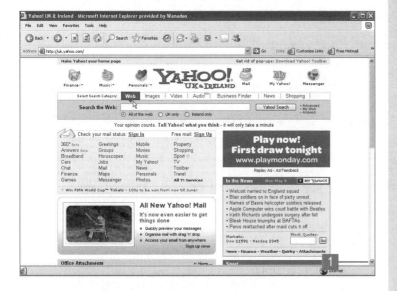

Submit your website details to Yahoo!

1 Yahoo! is a popular web portal or gateway as, in addition to the search facility, it enables viewers to browse by website category. Scroll right down to the bottom of the page and click on How to Suggest a Site.

Jargon buster

Search engine – a powerful software application that automatically retrieves information about web pages and delivers lists of links to relevant pages in response to keywords typed in by the user.

Submitting information to search engines (cont.)

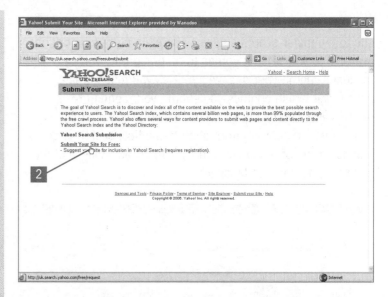

2 Click on Submit Your Site For Free.

3 Create a new account if you don't already have one with Yahoo!

For your information

It can take several weeks, even months, for your listing to appear on a portal as popular as Yahoo! But since this is a consequence of its popularity, you can be sure other web users are browsing regularly and will find your site eventually. And don't think you can outwit the service by sending in your site details over and over again. This can in fact have the opposite effect and lead to your site being blacklisted.

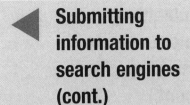

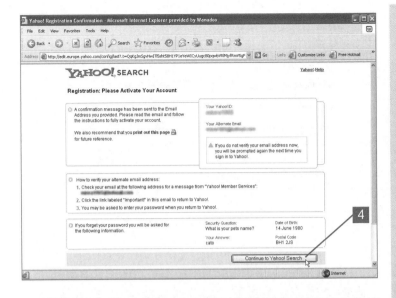

4 Your registration details are displayed. It is worth printing these out for future reference. Click on Continue to Yahoo! Search.

5 Submit the URLs of the pages you want included.

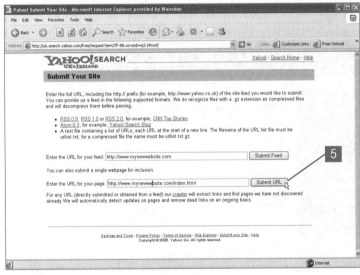

9

Submitting information to search engines (cont.)

6 Note that the Yahoo! search engine operates by automatically sifting through millions of pages worth of content every day using software programmes called web crawlers. These move from site to site via the links, searching the internet for new content and keywords and then categorising sites appropriately. Your site may therefore turn up on Yahoo! even if you don't submit it but you'll optimise your chances if you do.

Submitting your site to multiple search engines

1 We've opted to use Web CEO as there is a free version that you can explore to see if it suits your needs. The other good thing about this software is that it's easy to use with a simple set-up process.

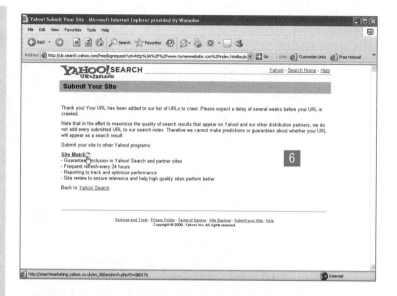

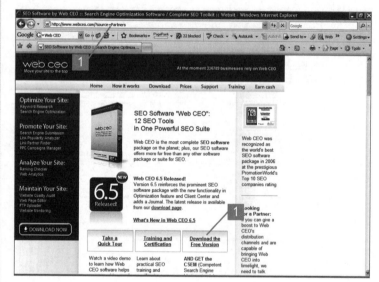

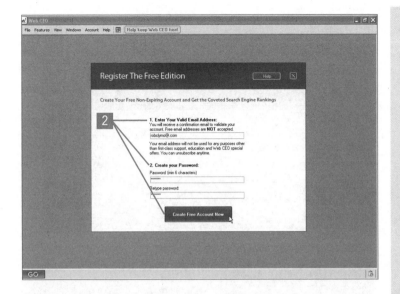

2 Install and register the product as directed.

3 Click on Add New Site to submit your website. You can add as many different sites as you like.

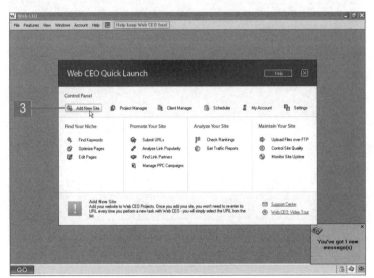

Did you know?

It can take weeks or even months for a search engine to start reflecting your website in its searches so don't expect instant success. However, some careful promotion and a regular site submission regime can improve your chances.

9

Submitting information to search engines (cont.)

4 Type in the URL of your site along with a short description and complete the Wizard.

See also

If you've created a hobby page that attracts viewers with a specific interest, it's a good idea to sign up to a 'webring'. See pages 32–33 in Chapter 2. This way you specifically select for visitors who are likely to be interested in your site.

Important

If you decide to use software to submit your site to the search engines then it's a good idea to have a spare email address at the ready. Most of these programs will need an email address when you register and this can result in a lot of spam. So it's worthwhile opening up a dedicated account for this – Hotmail is a good candidate as it reduces the risk of viruses and other unwanted junk contaminating your own PC.

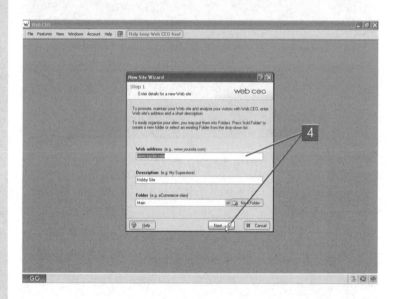

The QuickLaunch window allows you to carry out all manner of tasks relating to the upkeep of your website. Spend some time exploring the different features.

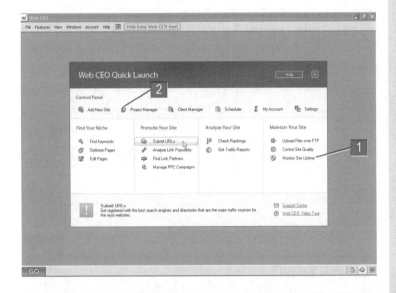

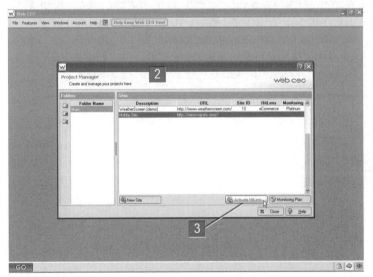

1. Monitor the Uptime of your site – i.e. find out the amount of time it is 'online' or being accessed by someone. If the Uptime is lower than you expect, it could be because you need to do some more site promotion, or it could be that there are problems with the server – a good indication of how dependable your web hosting company is.

2. For a wonderfully detailed analysis of the activity on your website, try the Project Manager feature.

3. Click on Activate HitLens to view a detailed analysis of the traffic on your site.

Timesaver tip

There is a handy little button in the top right-hand corner of the 'WeatherScreen' window. Simply click on Teach Me for information on how the software can help you.

Monitoring site activity with Web CEO (cont.)

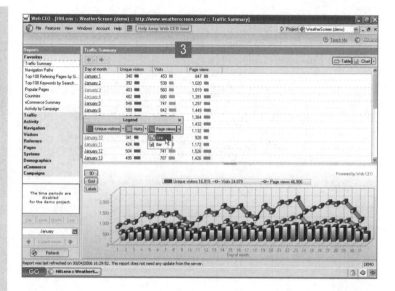

4 It is worth resubmitting your website to the search engines each time you do any major alterations so that the most up-to-date version is always being promoted.

Did you know?

Web CEO can keep you posted on all the latest activity at your website. When you login, you'll see a small green flag in the bottom right-hand corner of the Quick Launch window letting you know about new messages that contain information on your website statistics.

There's no getting away from the fact that it takes time for a website to get popular. One of the best ways of keeping tabs on how many new visitors view your site is to monitor your 'hits'. If you have signed up with a web hosting company, it is likely that providing information and statistics on the activity at your site is part of your package.

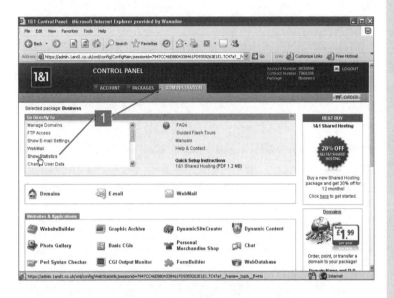

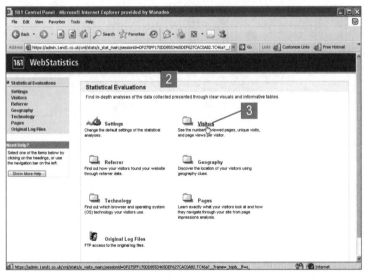

1 On the 1&1 Internet site, your statistics are accessed through the Administration tab.

2 Statistical Evaluations gives a good indication of data collected and where your visitors are based and which pages they are viewing.

9

Exploiting the visitor information captured by your web host (cont.)

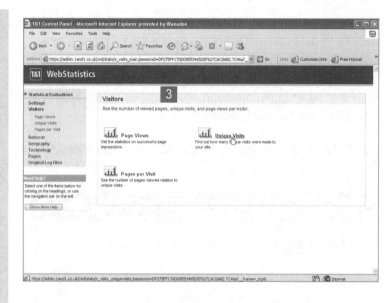

3 Click on Visitors to find out even more about their habits...

4 No point in indulging in too much navel gazing about why you get more visitors on a Tuesday until the variation is statistically significant!

For your information

You can customise the way the statistics are presented to help you analyse it better. Set your preferences by clicking on Settings in the Statistical Evaluations window.

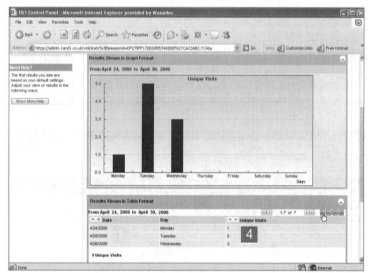

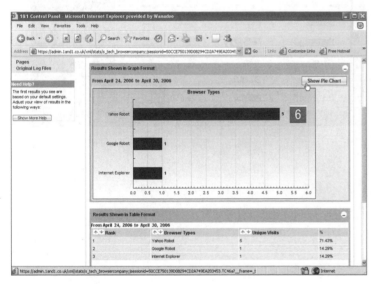

Exploiting the visitor information captured by your web host (cont.)

5 Finding out which browsers your readers are using will help you to ensure you are previewing new pages with the right ones to ensure your readers see what you want them to see.

6 The results can be surprising.

Did you know?

The great thing about these data capturing systems is that the information is available almost instantly. Taking a look at the activity soon after you have added some new pages or made major amendments will help you to track how popular your changes are.

9

Exploiting the visitor information captured by your web host (cont.)

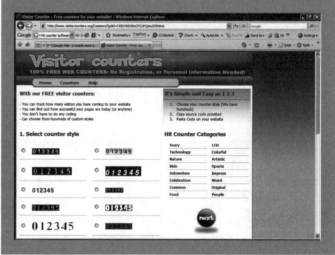

If you have some budget available for advertising, it is worth considering services such as Google AdWords. The service allows you to target your website at specific searchers – your site will be featured in the list of sponsored links that appears to the right-hand side of the results screen. And the cost-per-click pricing model means that you only pay when readers actually do click through to your site.

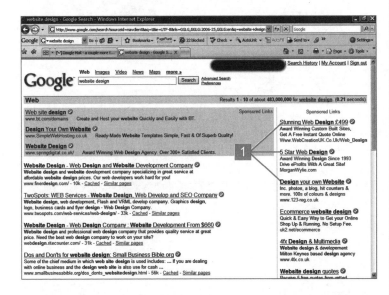

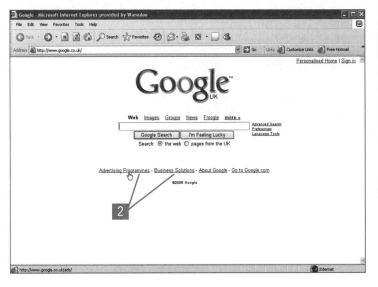

Advertising with AdWords

1. Notice the sponsored links that come up when you perform a search.

2. To sign up for the service, head to the Google home page, located at www.google.co.uk. Click on Advertising Programmes, or, if you are promoting a business, click on Business Solutions to explore Google's commercial services.

Did you know?

Google offers another service worth considering called AdSense. This is an extension of the AdWords philosophy which can present you with additional money-making opportunities because it allows you to display perfectly targeted advertisers on your own web pages, thereby generating interest and revenue for all concerned.

9

Advertising with AdWords (cont.)

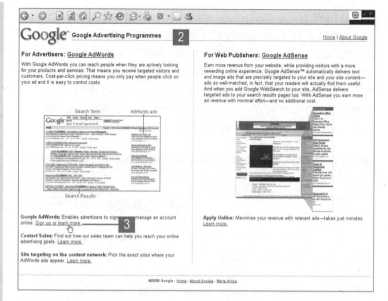

3 Click on Sign up or learn more.

4 One of the best things about the Google AdWords service is that it is very flexible and you can customise it to work the way you want. So it's worthwhile taking a quick tour of the various options available to you under Learn More.

5 Click on Click to begin to sign up.

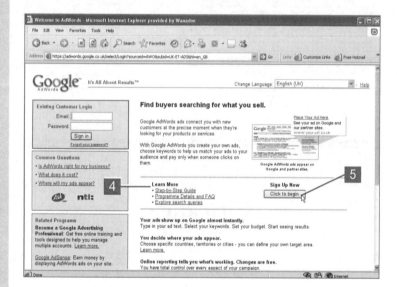

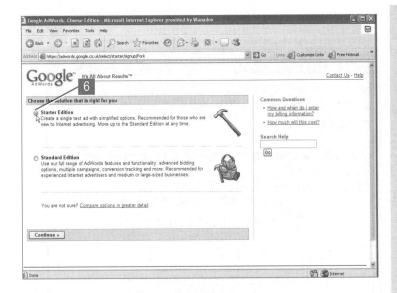

6 We will explore the Starter Edition.

7 Work through the signup wizard. You can go back and change your mind about any of the options you have chosen at any time up until you submit your billing information at the end.

? Did you know?

The service provides you with Editorial Guidelines to help you write the text of your advertisement as well as advice on selecting effective keywords.

! Important

You can stop your campaign at any time if you aren't happy with the results you're getting.

9

Advertising with AdWords (cont.)

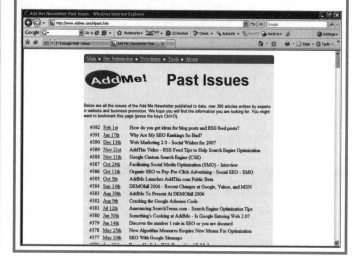

Jargon buster

ALT tags – textual descriptions of web page elements, such as images and icons, that appear when the user's mouse hovers over the element.

Bitmap – a simple graphics file format used by Microsoft Windows software.

Bookmark – a way of keeping a record of websites that you want to visit again. Your browser keeps a list of the URLs as 'your favourites' so you can easily return to them without having to remember the web addresses.

Browser – a software application especially designed for accessing and displaying the information in the web. This is also true the other way around: the web is an information system designed to be viewed on browsers.

CSS – short for Cascading Style Sheets – a style sheet language that is used to define the presentation of documents where the content is written in a mark up language, for example, HTML. The language defines all aspects of presentation such as fonts, colours, text sizes, layout, etc. The key feature of CSS is that in using it, you can separate the content of the web page from its presentation. This powerful tool has numerous benefits: it reduces the size and complexity of the document code by removing all the presentational elements, it provides the website designer with a very quick and easy way to change the style of an entire website in a

matter or clicks, it even allows the reader to change the way the content is presented to suit his/her needs (e.g. changing the layout to suit a smaller screen on a mobile phone).

Domain name – the part of an internet address that identifies the organisation it belongs to.

Download – copying files and other data from a remote computer to a local one.

Email – electronic mail – a system for sending messages and files across networks.

FAQs – Frequently Asked Questions – a list of the most common questions users of a website may pose. Referring to this section of the site is the first port of call if you don't understand something about the way it functions.

FTP – short for File Transfer Protocol – the method most usually used for transferring files across the internet.

GIF files – short for Graphics Interchange Format – graphics files that use a palette of up to 256 distinct colours to produce an image. This makes them ideal for images which use solid blocks of colour but unsuitable for colour photographs or images that use continuous colour.

Google – the world's most popular search engine.

Hard disk – the primary storage area for all the data on your computer.

Home page – the first page your browser loads when you type in the address or URL of a website. The 'gateway' or entrance to a site.

HTML – HyperText Markup Language, a system of instructions that browsers can interpret to display text and images.

Hyperlinks – connections between different web pages and websites made possible using URLs.

Hypertext – a dynamic form of cross-referencing that is used in web pages to allow the reader to simply 'click' through to the referenced document or file rather than having to look it up manually.

Image map – a picture with several hyperlinks attached to different areas so that the one picture can be the route to many places.

Index – the home page and entrance to your website. The first page to open when your web address is typed into a browser.

Internet – the global network of networked computers (**inter**connected **net**works) and the software systems that allow them to interact.

ISP – Internet Service Provider – organisation whose main business it is to enable people to access the internet.

JPEG – short for Joint Photographic Experts Group – the committee that developed the file format. It specifies the way that colours are transformed into bytes and is ideal for photographs and other continuous colour images.

Keywords – a hand-picked set of words that have relevance to a particular website. Used by automatic search engines to determine which pages match the user's search criteria.

Login – a request for your user name and associated password. This is the most common method of restricting access to certain information and websites.

Meta data – information written into the header section of HTML documents for the benefit of automatic software applications such as web crawlers that visit and read websites, but that is not visible on screen.

Personal home page – a web page focusing on an individual and his/her interests.

Pixel – tiny rectangular blocks of colour that together make up a digital image. Each pixel has a colour value that is defined as the specific blend of red, green and blue light it contains. Digital images are comprised of rows of pixels and the smaller each pixel is the more you need to fill the space. High resolution pictures contain very small pixels. Low resolution pictures contain larger pixels. The higher the resolution, the longer the picture will take to load.

PNG – short for Portable Network Graphics – this format was created to improve upon GIF. It was created specifically for transferring files on the internet so it supports the screen-friendly RGB colour palette and is not suitable for professional printing. It is ideal for line drawings, icons and other solid colour graphics as it preserves sharp edges and it is not limited to the 256 colours of GIF files.

Publish – putting your web pages online for others to see.

Raster layer – a line of pixels is called a raster so in a raster layers the data is comprised of individual pixels – great for continuous colour pictures and images such as photos.

Root – the name of the main folder or directory on your hard drive that holds all of the files and data destined for your website.

Search engine – a powerful software application that automatically retrieves information about web pages and delivers lists of links to relevant pages in response to keywords typed in by the user.

Server – a computer that provides services to other computers. A web server is a remote computer with which your computer communicates in order to access websites. Billions of servers house the data and information on the web.

Surfing – following hyperlinks from one website to another, also known as 'browsing'.

URL – Uniform Resource Locator – a standard way to identify the location of web pages and other documents that can be accessed via the web.

Vector layer – a layer where the data is comprised of the mathematical co-ordinates of the objects in the picture – great for sharply defined lines and shapes and perfect curves.

Web – World Wide Web, also shortened to WWW or W3. One of the most popular ways of using the internet, it consists of billions of web pages that can be viewed through browsers.

Web blog – an interactive online journal or diary or commentary on events and issues where content is provided both by the originator and the readers in the form of comments.

Web page – a document accessed using a web browser. It may be plain or formatted text and may hold pictures, sound files and videos.

Web page template – a pre-designed web page layout that can be adapted or customised for a particular use.

Web portal – a gateway or entrance to a selection of websites that may be categorised to help the user find sites he/she is interested in. Additional features are often added to encourage web users to use a specific portal as their default starting site when browsing, such as news feeds, search engine facilities and personalisation options.

Webring – a community of similarly themed websites that are linked so that users can navigate their way through them via a single 'hub'.

Web safe palette – a subset of commonly used colours that browsers display in a standard way. Colours not contained in this palette may not be viewed in the same way on different browsers.

Website – a set of related web pages, usually owned and constructed by one organisation or individual. Navigational aids and hyperlinks allow the visitor to find their way around the site.

Wizard – a part of the user interface that leads the user step-by-step through a complex task using a series of dialog boxes.

WYSIWYG – short for 'What You See Is What You Get'. A term applied to applications with user interfaces that allow you, the user, to edit your data in such a way that what you see on the screen as you work is an accurate reflection of the end result.

Troubleshooting guide

Navigation and linking pages

Problems